119 PRACTICAL PROGRAMS FOR THE TRS-80® POCKET COMPUTER

119 PRACTICAL PROGRAMS FOR THE TRS-80® POCKET COMPUTER

BY JOHN CLARK CRAIG

TAB BOOKS Inc.
BLUE RIDGE SUMMIT, PA. 17214

JONATHAN SPYRA OCT 5, 1982

FIRST EDITION

SECOND PRINTING

Printed in the United States of America

Library of Congress Cataloging in Publication Data

Craig, John Clark
119 practical programs for the TRS-80 pocket computer.

Includes index.
1. TRS-80 (Computer)—Programming. 2. Computer programs. I. Title. II. Title: One hundred nineteen practical programs for the TRS-eighty pocket computer.
QA76.8.T18C7 001.64'2 81-18262
ISBN 0-8306-0061-2 AACR2
ISBN 0-8306-1350-1 (pbk.)

Contents

Introduction

The TRS-80 Pocket Computer excellently fills the gap between handheld, programmable calculators and desktop computers! The BASIC computer language is easy to learn and powerful; an improvement over the non standard methods previously used for the various programmable calculators. And yet, the TRS-80 Pocket Computer is portable enough to be carried into the classroom, laboratory, and meetings, places where a real computer can be very useful.

It's almost an unwritten law that computer programs should be easy to read and as self explanatory as possible. Plenty of REMARK lines, single statements per line, and extra spaces help to achieve these goals in the BASIC language. For desktop computers this approach is appropriate; however, for the TRS-80 Pocket Computer a slightly different philosophy of program design is warranted.

This book presents a collection of immediately useful, efficient programs that will allow your TRS-80 Pocket Computer to provide you with quick results. The protected memory feature allows you to load several programs into memory and use them individually as necessary. The fewer steps that each program requires, the more computational power you can have loaded and ready to run!

Each program in this book has a label in the first line. And each program terminates with the statement GOTO 1. This is because a special two-line program has been designed to work with all the programs in this book. You may change each GOTO 1 statement to an END statement and ignore the labels if you prefer, but at least give this "driver" program a try! It's the very first program in the book, entitled All Purpose Driver.

These programs have been written very compactly. There are ways to squeeze them down even further if desired. Most of the prompting messages can be shortened, as can the program labels. These were not shortened too far for this book in order to keep the programs as understandable as possible. Unclosed parenthesis are allowed on your TRS-80 Pocket Computer. At the expense of readability you could save a few program steps by leaving them open.

This collection of programs is a sampling from many different areas of interest. Subjects include games, finance, electronics, statistics, engineering, numerical analysis, and others.

The programs cover a wide range of subjects. There should be programs of interest for just about everyone. The programming techniques and ideas presented will help you design and write other similar programs in your areas of interest.

Acknowledgments

I would like to take this opportunity to extend my thanks to the following people: my wife Jeanie for believing in me, Jennifer and John Adam for being great kids and keeping the television turned down, Bob Carroll for his photographic expertise, and the rest of my family and friends for their advice and encouragement.

Most of the illustrations in this book were drawn by some android friends of mine, HP9825A and HP9872A. Thank you both for your after-hours help. And, thank you Anaconda Company for letting them help me.

All-Purpose Driver ™

Though it is assumed that you have read your manual and are familiar with the operation of your pocket computer, this book will reiterate a few features that are quite useful, or that differ substantially from other BASICs.

To begin, segments of BASIC code can be labeled by enclosing the label name in quotes immediately after the line number. The label can be any phrase, but if it is a single letter that is reversible, then that segment of code can be executed from the DEF mode by merely typing SHFT and then typing the proper key. Using a key as a label does not prevent you from using it as a reserved word key, and in the RUN, PRO, and RESERVE modes SHFT and the same key will give you the reserved word instead of the branch to the labeled section. You can also say GOTO "label," but only in a program.

Remember that PRINT stops program execution, but using PAUSE instead displays the printout for about a second, and it then continues. USING can be used in the normal manner, to format output, but if it appears at the end of a statement, it clears the display mode.

The All-Purpose Driver™ acts as an operating system for BASIC. By ending your programs with GOTO 1, instead of END, and running your programs in the DEF mode, the computer will always return to this operating system at the end of a run, and you can start another program just by typing its label. You can even start the operating system itself by entering the DEF mode and typing SHFT =.

This program makes use of an interesting aspect of the INPUT statement. If the ENTER key is hit with no other input, the computer skips the rest of the program line and goes to the next line. This feature is not one usually found in BASIC.

Also note that the examples only show the ENTER key when you must hit it and nothing else. It is assumed that you know to hit it after each entry.

Every program in this book terminates with the statement GOTO 1. When a program ends, you'll immediately see the >>> in the display again. If you prefer to manually RUN your programs, replace the GOTO 1 statements with END, and erase program lines 1 and 2 from memory.

There is one important rule to remember when loading several programs into memory at the same time. Program line numbers must be changed to prevent conflict. The easiest way to do this is by adding a nice round constant amount to each line in a program. For instance, instead of lines 10, 20, and 30, number them 710, 720, and 730 for one program, and 810, 820, and 830 in another.

Occasionally you might need to do some calculations and wish to get away from the > > > prompt. Just press ENTER and the driver program will terminate. After your manual calculations are complete, press SHFT and = to return to the > > > prompt.

LISTING

```
1 " ="USING
  : INPUT" > > > ";Z$
  : GOTO Z$
2 END
```

Bernoulli Numbers

This program computes the Nth Bernoulli Number. For a small N, such as N=1 or N=2, the looping in line 20 will continue for a long time. Line 20 sums the terms of the expansion until a term is small enough that the sum doesn't change. Notice that the terms will get smaller more rapidly when N is large.
Here are the first three Bernoulli numbers:

B(1) = 1 / 6
B(2) = 1 / 30
B(3) = 1 / 42

For example, what is the 8th Bernoulli number?

Display	You Enter
>>>	B
?	8
7.092156862	ENTER
>>>	

Program length is 97 steps.

LISTING

```
10 "B" INPUT N
   : N=2N
   : I=0
   : X=0
20 I=I+1
   : Y=X
   : X=X+1 / I^N
   : IF X > Y THEN 20
30 M=1
   : FOR Z=2 TO N
   : M=MZ
   : NEXT Z
40 PRINT MX / ( ( π ^ N) * 2^(N-1))
   : GOTO 1
```

Bessel Functions

This pair of programs computes the Bessel functions Jn(X) and In(X).

BSLJ—Computes Jn(X) given n and X. Also computes J0(X) and J1(X).

BSLI—Computes In(X) given n and X.

Example: Compute J4(7. 8) and I3(4. 2).

Display	You Enter
> > >	BSLJ
FOR JN(X) N?	4
X?	7. 8
J4. (X)=−5.571870495 E−02	ENTER
J0 (X)=2.154078077 E−01	ENTER
J1 (X)=2.013568727 E−01	ENTER
> > >	BSLI
FOR IN(X) N?	3
X?	4. 2
I3. (X)= 4.211952206	ENTER
> > >	

Program length is 362 steps.

LISTING

```
10 "BSLJ" INPUT"FOR JN(X) N?",A,"X?",X
   : GOSUB 100
   : F=1
20 GOSUB 200
   : N=N+D
   : GOSUB 200
   : IF I GOTO 20
30 Q=2N−E
   : J=C / Q
   : K=E / Q
   : L=−D / Q
40 PRINT "J";A;"(X)=";J
50 PRINT "J0 (X)=";K
   : PRINT "J1(X)=";L
   : GOTO 1
60 "BSLI"INPUT"FOR IN(X) N?",A,"X?",X
   : F=0
```

```
   : GOSUB 100
 70 N=N+D
   : GOSUB 200
   : IF I THEN 70
 80 I=C / (2N−E)*EXP (2 / B)
   : PRINT "I";A;"(X)=";I
   : GOTO 1
100 C=3X / 2
   : T=A
   : IF C > A LET T=C
110 I=2+2*INT( (T+6+9C / (C+2)) / 2)
120 B=3 / C
   : E=0
   : N=0
   : D= E−9
   : RETURN
200 I=I−1
   : IF A=I LET C=D
210 T=E
   : IF F LET T=−T
220 E=D
   : D=T+IBE
   : RETURN
```

Black Holes

This program computes three of four quantities, relating to black holes in space, given any one known quantity. They are; mass in grams, Schwarzchild radius in centimeters, temperature in degrees Kelvin, and mean liftetime in seconds. Just press ENTER when asked for an unknown. For example: If the mass of the earth was suddenly converted into a black hole, what would it's Schwarzchild radius, temperature, and expected lifetime be?

Display	You Enter
>>>	BH
MASS? (GRAMS)	5.983*E*27
MASS= 5.9830*E*27 GM	ENTER
RADIUS= 8.8846*E*−01 CM	ENTER
TEMP= 1.6714*E*−02 K	ENTER
LIFE= 2.1416*E*55	ENTER
>>>	

Program length is 291 steps.

LISTING

```
 10 "BH"CLEAR
    : INPUT"MASS? (GRAMS)";M
    : GOTO 50
 20 INPUT"RADIUS? (CM)";R
    : GOTO 50
 30 INPUT"TEMP? (KELVIN)";K
    : GOTO 50
 40 INPUT"LIFETIME? (SEC)";L
 50 A=1.484986855E-28
    : IF R LET M=R / A
 60 IF L LET M=(L / E-28)^(1 / 3)
 70 IF K LET M=E26 / K
 80 R=MA
    : L=E-28M^3
    : K=E26 / M
    : USING"#.# # # #^"
 90 PRINT"MASS= ";M;" GM"
100 PRINT"RADIUS= ";R;" CM"
110 PRINT"TEMP= ";K;" K"
120 PRINT"LIFE= ";L;" SEC"
130 GOTO 1
```

Boolean Logic Truth Table

This program helps you construct a truth table for a Boolean algebra function of your design. You define your function beginning with program line 100. A single result must be returned in variable X. Variables A through V are available for use in the function. The input variables to the function should be sequential and start with A (A, B, and C for the three inputs of our example, for instance).

Because of the ability of your TRS-80 pocket computer to return a 1 for "true" and a 0 for "false," some clever programming steps easily define Boolean functions such as OR, AND, and NOT. For example, the program steps A=0=A provide a convenient NOT A function. If 0=A is true then A will contain 1 after this test, if 0 = A is false, A will contain 0. This statement then effectively computes NOT A.

Here are several Boolean logic functions expressed in TRS-80 logic form. The rule to remember is that any positive value is true and 0 is false.

AND	X=AB
OR	X=A+B
NOT	X=0=A
NAND	X=0=AB
NOR	X=0=A+B
XOR	X=(A+B)*(AB=0)

For example, let's construct a truth table for the logic circuit of Fig. 1. The equation for this circuit is

$$X=\bar{A}\bar{B}C+\bar{A}B\bar{C}+A\bar{B}\bar{C}+ABC$$

There are several ways to program this function using the TRS-80 logic as described. In this example the variables D, E, and F are first loaded with NOT A, NOT B, and NOT C. Then the final equation is formed from a combination of the variables A through F as in line 110. You must enter the proper number of inputs for the equation you develop; in this case 3.

Now that the function is programmed, we're ready to generate the truth table. (Fig. 2)

Display	You Enter
>>>	BOOL
NO. INPUTS?	3
INPUT # 1=	0
INPUT # 2=	0

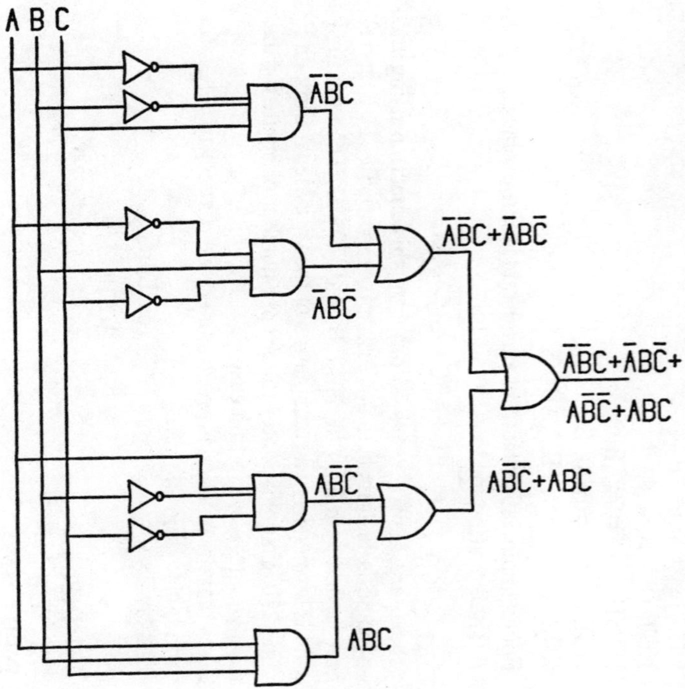

Fig. 1.

Logic Gates Truth Table

A	B	C	$\bar{A}\bar{B}C+\bar{A}B\bar{C}+A\bar{B}\bar{C}+ABC$
0	0	0	0
0	0	1	1
0	1	0	1
0	1	1	0
1	0	0	1
1	0	1	0
1	1	0	0
1	1	1	1

Fig. 2.

Display	You Enter
INPUT # 3=	0
X= 0	ENTER
INPUT # 1=	0
INPUT # 2=	0
INPUT # 3=	1
X= 1	ENTER
(etc.)	

The results should match the truth table in Fig. 2. Program length is 182 steps.

LISTING

```
 10 "BOOL" CLEAR
    : INPUT"NO. INPUTS?",Z
    : USING"###"
 20 GOSUB 100
    : FOR W=1 TO Z
    : PAUSE"INPUT #";W;"=";A(W)
    : NEXT W
 30 X=0 < X
    : PRINT" X=";X
    : Y=Z+1
 40 Y=Y-1
    : IF Y=0 GOTO 1
 50 A(Y)=0=A(Y)
    : IF A(Y) GOTO 20
 60 GOTO 40
100 D=0=A
    : E=0=B
    :F=0=C
110 X=DEC+DBF+AEF+ABC
    : RETURN
```

Calendar—Date

This program converts a date from its astronomical Julian day number to month, day, year format. You must also load the calendar subroutines DJ and JD for this program to work correctly. The accuracy range is from October 15, 1582 to February 28, 4000. Also computed is the day of the week for the given date. Example: What day of the week was July 4, 1776? And what is the astronomical Julian day number for this date? (Fig. 3)

Display	You Enter
>>>	DATE
MONTH?	7
DAY?	4
YEAR?	1776
M. D. Y.=7.4.1776.	ENTER
AST JULIAN #= 2369916.	ENTER
WEEKDAY (0=SU 6=SA) IS 4	ENTER
>>>	

Program length, including the necessary subroutines, is 454 steps including subroutines DJ and JD.

LISTING

```
10 "DATE"INPUT"MONTH?",M,"DAY?",D,"YEAR?",Y
   : GOSUB "DJ"
   : GOTO 30
20 INPUT"AST JULIAN #?", J
   : GOSUB "JD"
30 PRINT"M.D.Y. = ";M;D;Y
   : PRINT"AST JULIAN #= "; J
40 PRINT"WEEKDAY (0=SU 6=SA) IS ";W
   : GOTO 1
```

JULY 1776						
SUN	MON	TUE	WED	THU	FRI	SAT
	1	2	3	4	5	6
7	8	9	10	11	12	13
14	15	16	17	18	19	20
21	22	23	24	25	26	27
28	29	30	31			

Fig. 3.

Calendar—Easter

This program computes the date of Easter for a given year. The range of accuracy is from the year 1583 to the year 3999. You must also load the calendar subroutines DJ and JD for the program to work correctly.

For example: On what date will Easter Sunday be in the year 2106? (Fig. 4)

Display	You Enter
>>>	EASTER
YEAR?	2106
EASTER= 4.18.2106.	ENTER
>>>	

Program length, including the necessary subroutines, is 602 steps.

LISTING

```
200 "EASTER"INPUT"YEAR?",Y
    : A=Y / 19
    : A=Y-19*INT A+1
210 D=14*(A=1)+3*(A=2)+23*
    (A=3)+11*(A=4)+31*(A=5)+18*(A=6)
    : IF D GOTO 240
220 D=8*(A=7)+28*
    (A=8)+16*(A=9)+5*(A=10)+25*
    (A=11)+13*(A=12)
    : IF D GOTO 240
230 D=2*(A=13)+22*(A=14)+10*
    (A=15)+30*(A=16)+17*(A=17)+7*(A=18)
    +27*(A=19)
240 M=3+(D < 20)
    : GOSUB "DJ"
    : J=J+7-W
    : GOSUB "JD"
250 PRINT "EASTER = ";M;D;Y
    : GOTO 1
```

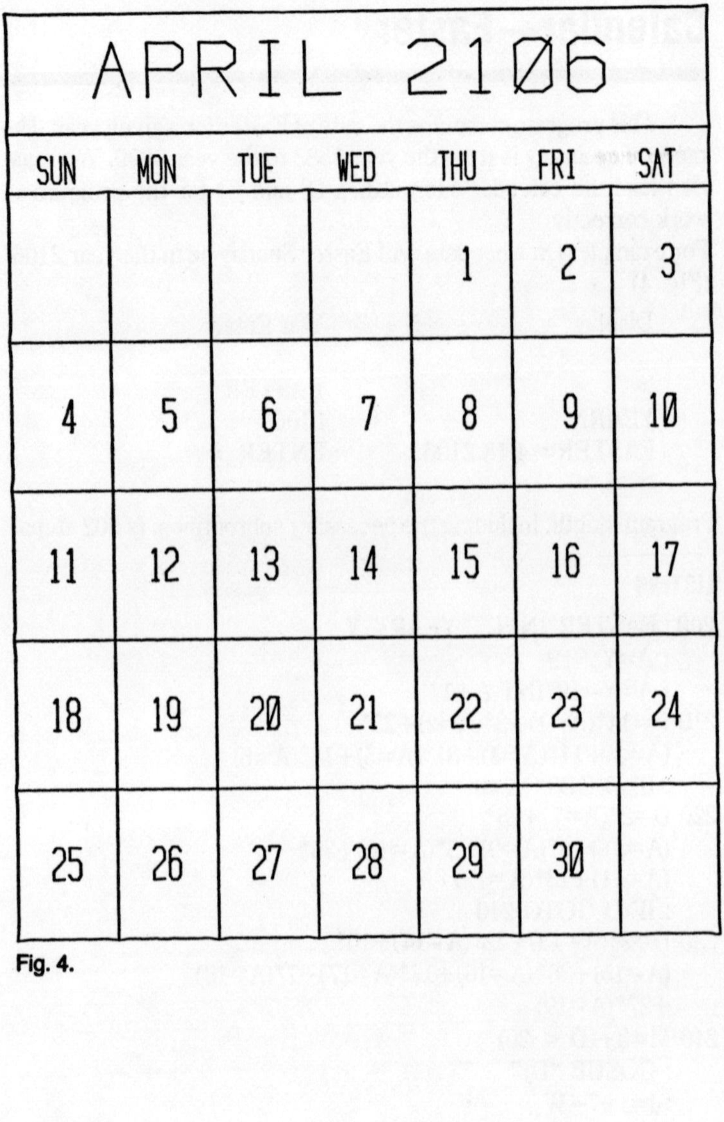
APRIL 21Ø6
SUN
MON
TUE
WED
THU
FRI
SAT
1
2
3
4
5
6
7
8
9
1Ø
11
12
13
14
15
16
17
18
19
2Ø
21
22
23
24
25
26
27
28
29
3Ø
Fig. 4.

Calendar—Moon

This program computes the phase of the moon for any date in the range of October 15, 1582 to February 28, 4000. You must also load the calendar subroutine DJ for this program to work correctly. For example: Describe the moon on June 25, 1982. (Fig. 5)

Display	You Enter
>>>	MOON
DATE M?	6
D?	25
Y?	1982
MOON LIT ABOUT 0.27	ENTER
HEADED FOR A NEW MOON.	ENTER
>>>	

Program length, including the necessary subroutine, is 349 steps.

LISTING

```
100 "MOON"INPUT"DATE M?",M,"D?",D,"Y?",Y
    : GOSUB "DJ"
110 M=(J+4.867) / 29.53058
    : M=2*(M-INT M)-1
    : N=ABS M
120 USING"##.##"
    : PRINT"MOON LIT ABOUT ";N
130 Z$="NEW"
    : IF M LET Z$="FULL"
140 PRINT"HEADED FOR A ";Z$;" MOON."
    : GOTO 1
```

Moon Phase

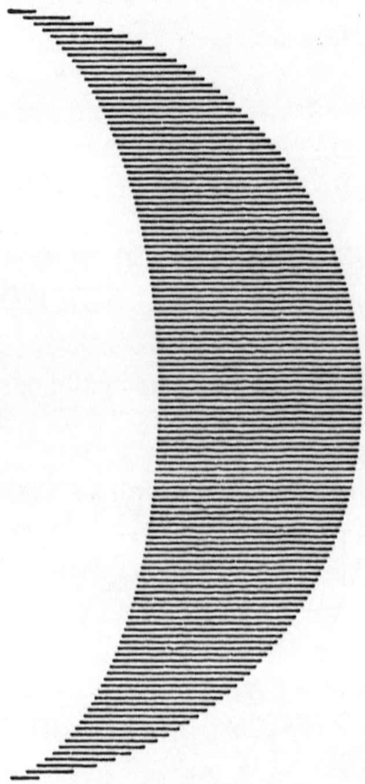

"MOON LIT ABOUT .27"
"HEADED FOR A NEW MOON."

Fig. 5.

Calendar—Subroutines

These subroutines are used by several calendar-related programs in this book.

DJ—Converts a date expressed as month, day, and year in variables M, D, and Y to the equivalent astronomical Julian day number. This day number is returned in variable J.

JD—Converts an astronomical Julian day number in variable J to the equivalent month, day, and year for that date. Variables M, D, and Y are returned with these values.

Both subroutines also return the day of the week in variable W. 0 for Sunday, 1 for Monday, and so on through 6 for Saturday.

These subroutines are quite powerful for many calendar related computations. The number of days between dates can be found by subtracting their astronomical Julian day numbers. A date's validity can be checked by calling first "DJ" and then "JD" and comparing the resulting values of M, D, and Y with the original values.

The range of accuracy is from October 15, 1582 (the day the Gregorian calendar began) to February 28, 4000. Be careful with dates earlier than the 1700s, however, as some countries were using calendars that differed by several days from each other. Program length is 303 steps.

LISTING

```
900 "DJ"J=INT(365.2422Y+30.44*(M-1)+D+1)
    : N=M-2+12*(M < 3)
905 Z=Y-(M < 3)
    : E=INT (Z / 100)
    : Z=Z-100E
910 W=INT(2.61N-.2)+D+Z+INT(Z / 4)+INT(E / 4)-2E
915 W=W-7*INT(W / 7)
    : X=J-7*INT(J / 7)
920 J=J-X+W-7*(X < W)+1721061
    : RETURN
950 "JD"G=J
    : Y=INT ( (J-1721061) / 365.25+1)
    : M=1
    : D=1
```

```
955 GOSUB "DJ"
    : IF J > G LET Y=Y-1
    : GOTO 955
960 M=INT ( (G-J) / 29+1)
965 GOSUB "DJ"
    : IF J > G LET M=M-1
    : GOTO 965
970 D=G-J+1
    : GOTO "DJ"
```

Calendar—Two Dates

This program may be used in two ways. If you input two dates the number of days between them will be computed. Or, if you input a date and a number of days to add to it, the second date will be computed. Accuracy range is from October 15, 1582, to February 28, 4000.

Example: How many days until Christmas on November 16, 1982?

Display	You Enter
>>>	2DATES
FIRST DATE M1?	11
D1?	16
Y1?	1982
2ND DATE M2?	12
D2?	25
Y2?	1982
39. DAYS BETWEEN	ENTER
>>>	

Program length is 494 steps.

LISTING

```
50 "2DATES"INPUT"FIRST DATE M1?",M,"D1?",D,"Y1?",Y
   : GOSUB "DJ"
60 A=J
   : INPUT"2ND DATE M2?",M, "D2?",D,"Y2?",Y
   : GOSUB "DJ"
   : GOTO 90
70 INPUT"# DAYS FROM DATE?",N
   : J=J+N
   :GOSUB "JD"
80 PRINT"NEW M.D.Y.=";M;D;Y
   : GOTO 1
90 PRINT J-A;"DAYS BETWEEN"
   : GOTO 1
```

Checkbook

This program will help you balance your checkbook. Start by entering the beginning balance. Then, for every check or deposit that has cleared the bank (is listed in the bank statement) enter the amount when asked. To bypass any questions, just press ENTER. An uncleared check or deposit is one that you have written down in your checkbook but is not noted on the bank statement. To see the balance so far, bypass all the questions until the balances are shown. The program will always branch back to the "CHECK?" question

Display	You Enter
>>>	CHECKS
BEGINNING BALANCE?	100
CHECK?	25
CHECK?	ENTER
DEPOSIT?	10
CHECK?	ENTER
DEPOSIT?	ENTER
UNCLEARED CHECK?	60
CHECK?	ENTER
DEPOSIT?	ENTER
UNCLEARED CHECK?	ENTER
UNCLEARED DEPOSIT?	ENTER
BEEP	
BOOK SHOULD SAY 25.00	ENTER
BEEP	
BANK SHOULD SAY 85.00	ENTER
CHECK?	(etc.)

Program length is 243 steps.

LISTING

```
10 "CHECKS"USING"# # # # # # . # #"
   : INPUT"BEGINNING BALANCE?",A
   : B=A
20 INPUT"CHECK? ";C
   : A=A-C
   : B=B-C
   : GOTO 20
30 INPUT"DEPOSIT? ";D
   : A=A+D
```

```
    : B=B+D
    : GOTO 20
40 INPUT "UNCLEARED CHECK? ";E
    : A=A−E
    : GOTO 20
50 INPUT"UNCLEARED DEPOSIT? ";F
    : A=A+F
    : GOTO 20
60 BEEP 1
    : PRINT"BOOK SHOULD SAY";A
70 BEEP 1
    : PRINT"BANK SHOULD SAY";B
    : GOTO 20
```

Chi-Square

This program computes the Chi-square statistic for a group of observed frequencies and their expected frequencies.

Example: Compute the Chi-square statistic for the following data.

Observed frequency	6	12	15
Expected frequency	10	10	10

Display	You Enter
>>>	CHI
OBS FREQ?	6
EXP FREQ?	10
OBS FREQ?	12
EXP FREQ?	10
OBS FREQ?	15
EXP FREQ?	10
OBS FREQ?	ENTER
CHI^2= 4.5	ENTER
>>>	

Program length is 76 steps.

LISTING

```
10 "CHI"CLEAR
20 INPUT"OBS FREQ?",X,"EXP FREQ?",E
   : A=A+XX / E-2X+E
   : GOTO 20
30 PRINT"CHI^2= ";A
   : GOTO 1
```

Circle—Determined By Three X, Y Points

This program computes and describes a circle that passes through three given X, Y points. For example: What circle passes through the points (3, 12), (10, 13), and (7, 4)? (Fig. 6)

Display	You Enter
>>>	CIR
X1?	3
Y1?	12
X2?	10
Y2?	13
X3?	7
Y3?	4
RADIUS= 5.	ENTER
CENTER (X,Y) – >	ENTER
7. 9.	ENTER
AREA= 78.53981634	ENTER
>>>	

Program length is 243 steps.

LISTING

```
10 "CIR"INPUT"X1?",A,"Y1?",B,"X2?",
   C,"Y2?",D,"X3?",E,"Y3?",F
20 K=(EE+FF–AA–BB) / 2 / (E–A)
   : L=(EE+FF–CC–DD) / 2 / (E–C)
30 N=(B–F) / (A–E)
   : P=(D–F) / (C–E)
   : Y=(L–K) / (P–N)
   : X=L–PY
   : T=C–X
   : U=D–Y
   : R= √(TT+UU)
   : V=πRR
40 PRINT"RADIUS= ";R
   : PRINT"CENTER (X,Y) – > "
50 PRINT X, Y
   : PRINT"AREA= ";V
   : GOTO 1
```

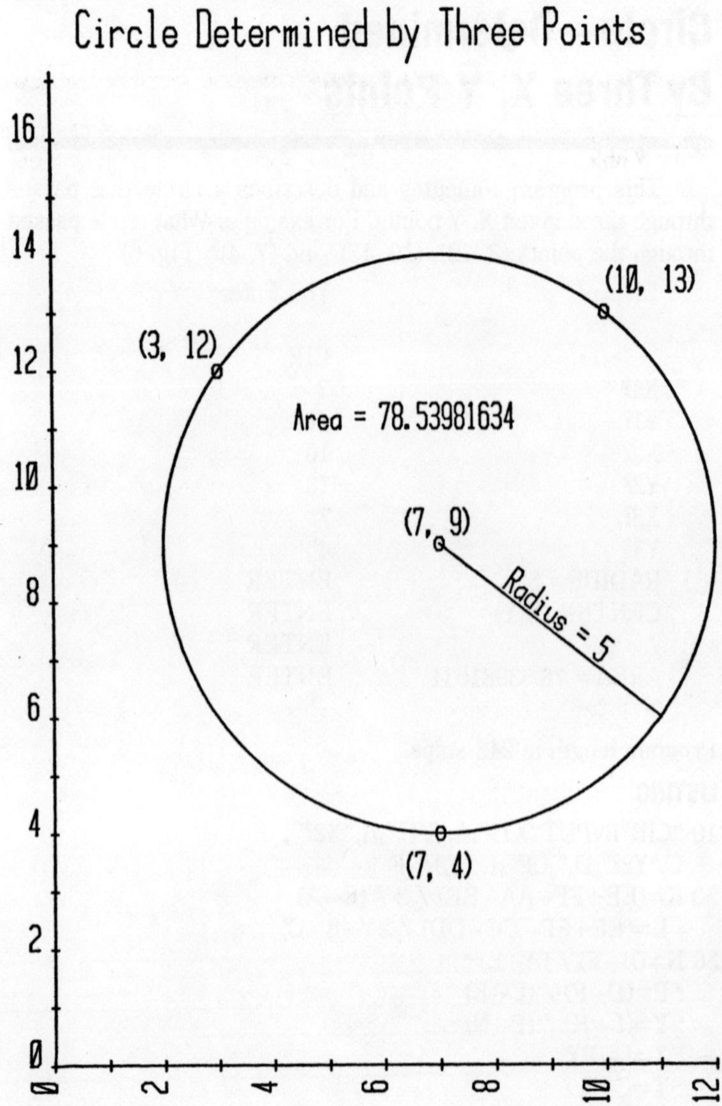

Circle Determined by Three Points
16
14
12
10
8
6
4
2
0
0
2
4
6
8
10
12
(10, 13)
(3, 12)
Area = 78.53981634
(7, 9)
Radius = 5
(7, 4)

Fig. 6.

Combinations

This program computes the number of combinations possible from Y objects taken X at a time. For example: How many combinations of 5 objects taken 3 at a time are possible? (Fig. 7)

Display	You Enter
>>>	CO
?	5
?	3
10.	ENTER
>>>	

Program length is 71 steps.

LISTING

```
10 "CO"INPUT Y,X
   : C=Y
   : IF Y-X > X LET X=Y-X
20 FOR Z=1 TO X
   : C=C / Z
   : IF Y-Z > Y-X LET C=CY-CZ
30 NEXT Z
   : PRINT C
   : GOTO 1
```

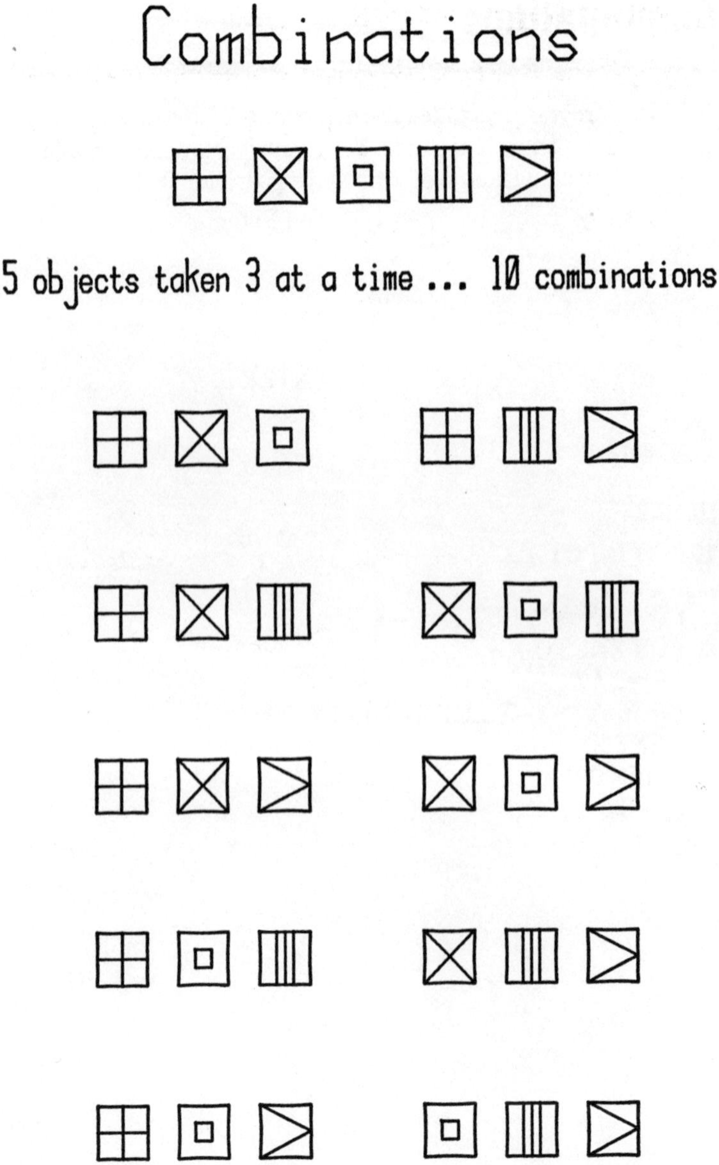

Fig. 7.

Complex Number Functions

This is a collection of nine programs for complex number analysis. A sample run of each program will help clarify their use.

C+	(A1+iB1) + (A2+iB2)
C–	(A1+iB1) – (A2+iB2)
C*	(A1+iB1) * (A2+iB2)
C /	(A1+iB1) / (A2+iB2)
1 / C	1 / (A+iB)
RP	(A+iB) converted to (R,A). "Rectangular to Polar".
PR	(R, A) converted to (A+iB). "Polar to Rectangular".
C2	(A+iB) squared.
√C	Square root of (A+1B).

Results are always returned in variables A and B. To use the results in a computation enter A when asked for A1?, and B when asked for B1?. This is demonstrated in some of the examples.

Compute (3+i4) + (2–i7).

Display	You Enter
>>>	C+
A1?	3
B1?	4
A2?	2
B2?	−7
5. −3.	ENTER
>>>	

The answer is (5–i3). Now subtract 3 from this result.

Display	You Enter
>>>	C–
A1?	A
B1?	B
A2?	3
B2?	0
2. −3.	ENTER
>>>	

The answer is (2–i3).

Compute 12 * (3+i4).

Display	You Enter
> > >	C*
A1?	0
B1?	2
A2?	3
B2?	4
−8. 6.	ENTER
> > >	

The answer is (−8+i6).
Compute (8−i6) / (3+i4).

Display	You Enter
> > >	C /
A1?	8
B1?	−6
A2?	3
B2?	4
0. −2	ENTER
> > >	

The answer is (−i2).
Compute 1 / (3+i4).

Display	You Enter
> > >	1 / C
A?	3
B?	4
0.12 −0.16	ENTER (.12−i.16) is the answer
> > >	"1 / C" (Let's check our answer.)
A?	A
B?	B
3. 4.	ENTER (Looks good.)
> > >	

Convert (3+i4) to polar notation, then back to rectangular. DEG mode is set.

Display	You Enter
> > >	RP
A?	3
B?	4
5. 53.13010235	ENTER

Display	You Enter
>>>	PR
A?	5
B?	53.13010235
3. 4.	ENTER
>>>	

Compute (3–i4) * (3–i4), then find the square root of the result.

Display	You Enter
>>>	C2
A?	3
B?	–4
–7. –24.	ENTER (–7–i24)
>>>	√C
A?	A
B?	B
3. 4.	ENTER
>>>	

Program length is 502 steps.

LISTING

```
10 "C+"GOSUB 200
   : A=A+C
   : B=B+D
   : GOTO 250
20 "C–"GOSUB 200
   : A=A–C
   : B=B–D
   : GOTO 250
30 "C*"GOSUB 200
   : A(27)=AC–BD
   : B=AD+BC
   : A=A(27)
   : GOTO 250
40 "C / "GOSUB 200
   : A(27)=AC+BD
   : A(28)=CC+DD
   : B=(BC–AD) / A(28)
   : A=A(27) / A(28)
   : GOTO 250
50 "1 / C"GOSUB 230
   : A(27)=AA+BB
```

```
   : A=A / A(27)
   : B=-B / A(27)
   : GOTO 250
60 "RP"GOSUB 230
   : A(27)= √(AA+BB)
   : A=(28)=ACS(A / A(27))
65 B=A(28)*SGN B+A(28)*(B=0)
   : A=A(27)
   : GOTO 250
70 "PR"GOSUB 230
   : A(27)=A*COS B
   : B=A*SIN B
   : A=A(27)
   : GOTO 250
80 "C2"GOSUB 230
   : A(27)=AA-BB
   : B=2AB
   : A=A(27)
   : GOTO 250
90 " √C"GOSUB 230
   : A= √( (A+ √(AA+BB)) / 2)
   : B=B / A / 2
   : GOTO 250
200 INPUT"A1?",A,"B1?",B
210 INPUT"A2?",C,"B2?",D
220 RETURN
230 INPUT"A?",A,"B?",B
240 RETURN
250 PRINT A,B
   : GOTO 1
```

Complex Numbers—Simultaneous Equations, Size Two

This program solves a pair of simultaneous equations for the two complex unknowns. Example: Solve for X and Y.

$$(1+i2)X + Y = (4-i)$$
$$(-i)X + (2+i3)Y = 1$$

Rewritten . . .

$$(1+i2)X + (1+i0)Y = (4-i1)$$
$$(0-i1)X + (2+i3)Y = (1+i0)$$

Display	You Enter
>>>	CSE2
REAL?	1
IMAG?	2
REAL?	1
IMAG?	0
REAL?	4
IMAG?	−1
REAL?	0
IMAG?	−1
REAL?	2
IMAG?	3
REAL?	1
IMAG?	0
0.5 −1.5	ENTER
0.5 −0.5	ENTER
>>>	

Or, X = (.5–i1.5) and Y = (.5–i.5)
Program length is 215 steps.

LISTING

```
10 "CSE2"FOR X=1 TO 6
   : Z=2X
   : Y=Z-1
   : INPUT"REAL?",A(Y),"IMAG?",A(Z)
   : NEXT X
20 M=AI-BJ-CG+DH
   : N=AJ+BI-CH-DG
```

```
   :O=EI−FJ−CK+DL
   :P=EJ+FI−CL−DK
30 Q=AK−BL−EG+FH
   : R=AL+BK−EH−FG
   : S=MM+NN
   : T=OM / S+PN / S
   U=PM / S−ON / S
40 PRINT T,U
   : V=QM / S+RN / S
   : W=RM / S−QN / S
   : PRINT V,W
   : GOTO 1
```

Coordinate Systems for Three Dimensions

This program translates coordinates in space between all three commonly used coordinate systems. (Fig. 8) There are three labels to activate this program.

REC—If the given coordinates are in rectangular notation, (X, Y, Z).
CYL—If the given coordinates are in cylindrical notation, (R, Theta, Z).
SPH—If the given coordinates are in spherical notation. (Rho, Theta, Phi).

Any angular mode is okay to use. For example: Convert the rectangular coordinates (3, 4, 5) to the other coordinates systems. DEG mode is set.

Display	You Enter
>>>	REC
X?	3
Y?	4
Z?	5
REC – >	ENTER
X=3.	ENTER
Y=4	ENTER
Z=5.	ENTER
CYL – >	ENTER
R= 5.	ENTER
THETA= 53.13010235	ENTER
Z= 5.	ENTER
SPH – >	ENTER
RHO= 7.071067812	ENTER
THETA= 53.13010235	ENTER
PHI= 45.	ENTER
>>>	

Program length is 350 steps.

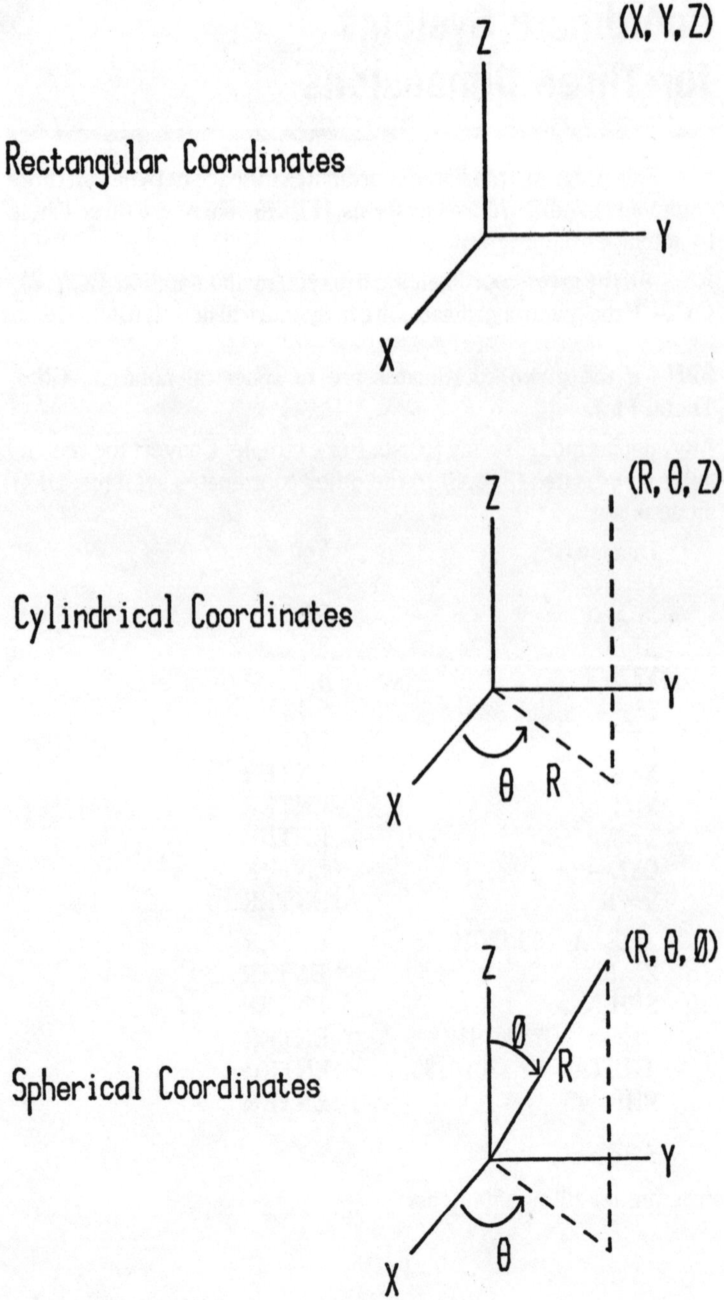
Rectangular Coordinates
(X, Y, Z)
Z
Y
X
Cylindrical Coordinates
(R, θ, Z)
Z
Y
X
θ
R
Spherical Coordinates
(R, θ, Ø)
Z
Ø
R
Y
X
θ

Fig. 8.

LISTING

```
 10 "CYL"INPUT"R?",R,"THETA?",T,"Z?",C
 20 X=R*COS T
    : Y=R*SIN T
    : GOTO 200
 30 "SPH"INPUT"RHO?",H,"THETA?",T, "PHI?",P
 40 X=H*COS T*SIN P
    : Y=H*SIN T*SIN P
    : C=H*COS P
    : GOTO 200
 50 "REC"INPUT"X?",X,"Y?",Y,"Z?",C
200 R=√(XX+YY)
    : T=ACS(X / R)
    : T=T*SGN Y+T*(Y=0)
210 H=√(XX+YY+CC)
    : P=ACS(C / H)
220 PRINT"REC – >"
    : PRINT"X= ";X
    : PRINT"Y= ";Y
    : PRINT"Z= ";C
230 PRINT"CYL – > "
    : PRINT"R= ";R
    : PRINT"THETA= ";T
    : PRINT"Z= ";C
240 PRINT"SPH –>"
    : PRINT"RHO= ";H
    : PRINT"THETA= ";T
    : PRINT"PHI= ";P
250 GOTO 1
```

Coordinate Translation / Rotation

This program translates X, Y points from an old coordinate system to a new coordinate system. The origin of the new coordinate system, expressed as a point in the old system, and the angular rotation of the systems relative to each other are first input. Then, for every X, Y point from the old coordinate system, the translated X, Y equivalent point in the new system is computed.

Example: A new coordinate system has it's origin at (9, 14) and is rotated 20 degrees as measured in the old coordinate system. (Fig. 9) What are the new coordinates for the point (17, 25)?

Display	You Enter
>>>	CTR
FOR NEW ORIGIN, X?	9
Y?	14
ROTATION ANGLE?	20
OLD X?	17
Y?	25
11.27976254 7.600457683	ENTER
OLD X?	ENTER
>>>	

Program length is 127 steps.

LISTING

```
10 "CTR"INPUT"FOR NEW ORIGIN, X?",A,"Y?",B,"ROTATION
   ANGLE?",R
   : S=SIN R
   : K=COS R
20 INPUT"OLD X?",X,"Y?",Y
   : D=AS-XS+YK-BK
   : PRINT XK-AK+YS-BS, D
   : GOTO 20
30 GOTO 1
```

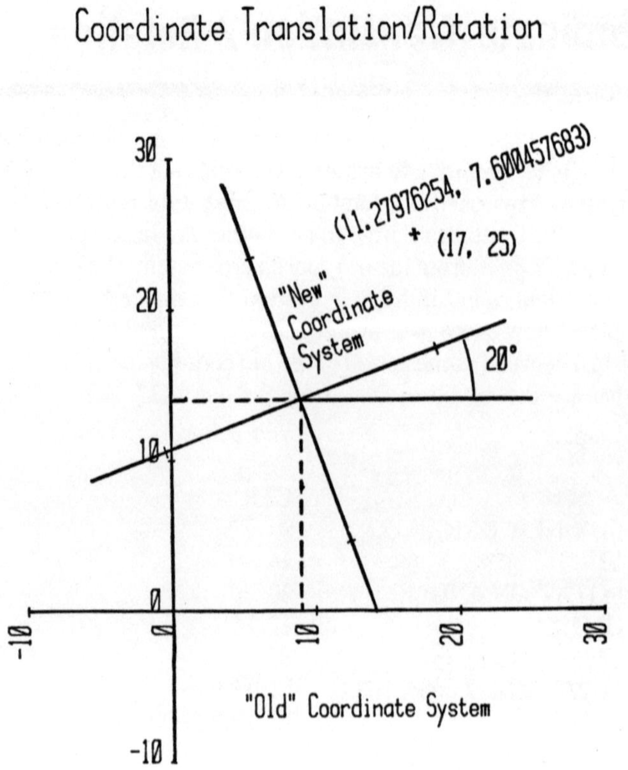
Coordinate Translation/Rotation
(11.27976254, 7.600457683)
(17, 25)
"New" Coordinate System
20°
30
20
10
0
-10
-10
0
10
20
30
"Old" Coordinate System

Fig. 9.

Cubic Equations

This program computes the real or complex roots of a cubic equation. For example: Compute the roots for X^3 +5X^2 – 2X – 24 = 0

Display	You Enter
>>>	CUB
AX^3+BX^2+CX+D=0	ENTER
A?	1
B?	5
C?	–2
D?	–24
REAL ROOT= 2.	ENTER
REAL ROOT= –4.	ENTER
REAL ROOT= –3.	ENTER
>>>	

Program length is 405 steps.

LISTING

```
10 "CUB"PRINT"AX^3+BX^2+CX+D=0"
   : INPUT"A?",A,"B?",B,"C?",C,"D?",D
20 Q=(3C–BB / A) / 9A
   : R=(9BC / A–27D–2BBB / A / A) / 54A
   : U=QQQ+RR
30 IF U > =0 LET P=1 / 3
   : S=R+ √U
   : S=SGN S*ABS S^P
   : T=R– √U
   : T=SGN T*ABS T^P
   : G=S+T–B / 3 / A
   : GOTO 50
40 Q=–Q
   : G=2* √Q*COS(ACS(R / √QQQ) / 3)–B / 3 / A
50 PRINT"REAL ROOT= ";G
   : E=G+B / A
   : C=GG+GB / A+C / A
   : B=E
   : A=1
```

```
60 D=(BB−4AC) / 4 / AA
   : E=−B / 2 / A
   : F= √ABS D
70 IF DLET S=E−F
   : Z=E+F
   : PRINT"REAL ROOT= ";S
   : PRINT"REAL ROOT= ";Z
   : GOTO 1
80 PRINT"COMPLEX ROOTS FOLLOW"
   : PRINT"REAL PART= ";E
   : PRINT"+ / − (I) = ";F
   : GOTO 1
```

Curve Fit—Exponential

This program uses the least squares method to fit an exponential equation (Y=A*EXP (BX)) to a set of given X,Y points. Example: Fit an exponential curve to the following data.

X .1 .7 1.2
Y 3.66 12.2 33.1

Display	You Enter
>>>	CFE
BEEP	
X?	.1
Y?	3.66
BEEP	
X?	.7
Y?	12.2
BEEP	
X?	1.2
Y?	33.1
BEEP	
X?	ENTER
Y=A*EXP(BX)	ENTER
A=2.998519512	ENTER
B= 2.002038184	ENTER
R^2= .9999977889	ENTER
NEW X?	1
22.20143341	ENTER
NEW X?	ENTER
>>>	

Program length is 202 steps.

LISTING

```
10 "CFE"CLEAR
20 BEEP 1
   : INPUT"X?",X,"Y?",Y
   : Y=LN Y
   : C=C+X
   : D=D+XX
   : E=E+Y
```

```
   : F=F+YY
   : G=G+XY
   : I =I+1
   : GOTO 20
30 J=GI-CE
   : B=J / (DI-CC)
   : A=EXP ((E-BC) / I)
   : R=BJ / (FI-EE)
40 PRINT"Y=A*EXP (BX)"
   : PRINT"A= ";A
   : PRINT"B= ";B
   : PRINT"R^2= ";R
50 INPUT"NEW X?",X
   : PRINT A*EXP BX
   : GOTO 50
60 GOTO 1
```

Curve Fit—Geometric

This program uses the least squares method to fit a geometric equation (Y=A*X^B) to a set of given X, Y points.
Example: Fit a geometric curve to the following data.

X	1.5	1.6	1.7	1.8
Y	2.1	1.7	1.4	1.2

Display	You Enter
>>>	CFG
BEEP	
X?	1.5
Y?	2.1
BEEP	
X?	1.6
Y?	1.7
BEEP	
X?	1.7
Y?	1.4
BEEP	
X?	1.8
Y?	1.2
BEEP	
X?	ENTER
Y=A*X^B	ENTER
A=7.287529642	ENTER
B=−3.086087334	ENTER
R^2= .9981553113	ENTER
NEW X?	1.4
2.579980683	ENTER
NEW X?	ENTER
>>>	

Program length is 203 steps.

LISTING

```
10 "CFG"CLEAR
20 BEEP 1
   : INPUT"X?",X,"Y?",Y
```

```
   : X=LN X
   : Y=LN Y
   : C=C+X
   : D=D+XX
   : E=E+Y
   : F=F+YY
   : G=G+XY
   : I=I+1
   : GOTO 20
30 J=GI-CE
   : B=J / (DI-CC)
   : A=EXP ((E-BC) / I)
   : R=BJ / (FI-EE)
40 PRINT"Y=A*X^B"
   : PRINT"A= ";A
   : PRINT"B= ";B
   : PRINT"R^2= ";R
50 INPUT"NEW X?",X
   : PRINT A*X^B
   : GOTO 50
60 GOTO 1
```

Curve Fit—Linear

This program uses the least squares method to fit a linear equation (Y=A+BX) to a set of given X,Y points.
Example: Fit a linear curve to the following data.

X	1	2	3
Y	1	1.9	3.1

Display	You Enter
> > >	CFL
BEEP	
X?	1
Y?	1
BEEP	
X?	2
Y?	1.9
BEEP	
X?	3
Y?	3.1
BEEP	
X?	ENTER
Y=A+BX	ENTER
A= −0.1	ENTER
B= 1.05	ENTER
R^2= .9932432432	ENTER
NEW X?	4
4.1	ENTER
NEW X?	ENTER
> > >	

Program length is 188 steps.

LISTING

```
10 "CFL"CLEAR
20 BEEP 1
  : INPUT"X?",X,"Y?",Y
  : C=C+X
  : D=D+XX
  : E=E+Y
  : F=F+YY
  : G=G+XY
```

```
   : I=I+1
   : GOTO 20
30 J=GI-CE
   : B=J / (DI-CC)
   : A=(E-BC) / I
   : R=BJ / (FI-EE)
40 PRINT"Y=A+BX"
   : PRINT"A= ";A
   : PRINT"B= ";B
   : PRINT"R^2= ";R
50 INPUT"NEW X?",X
   : PRINT A+BX
   : GOTO 50
60 GOTO 1
```

Curve Fit—Logarithmic

This program uses the least squares method to fit a logarithmic equation (Y=A+B*LN X) to a set of given X,Y points.
Example: Fit a logarithmic curve to the following data.

X	1	2	3	4
Y	5	7.8	9.4	10

Display	You Enter
>>>	CFLN
BEEP	
X?	1
Y?	5
BEEP	
X?	2
Y?	7.8
BEEP	
X?	3
Y?	9.4
BEEP	
X?	4
Y?	10
BEEP	
X?	ENTER
Y=A+B*LN X	ENTER
A= 5.109167233	ENTER
B= 3.701425997	ENTER
R^2= .9909435456	ENTER
NEW X?	5
11.06638256	ENTER
NEW X?	ENTER
>>>	

Program length is 200 steps.

LISTING

```
10 "CFLN"CLEAR
20 BEEP 1
   : INPUT"X?",X,"Y?",Y
```

```
    : X=LN X
    : C=C+X
    : D=D+XX
    : E=E+Y
    : F=F+YY
    : G=G+XY
    : I=I+1
    : GOTO 20
30 J=GI-CE
    : B=J / (DI-CC)
    : A=(E-BC) / I
    : R=BJ / (FI-EE)
40 PRINT"Y=A+B*LN X"
    : PRINT"A= ";A
    : PRINT"B= ";B
    : PRINT"R^2= ";R
50 INPUT"NEW X?",X
    : PRINT A+B*LN X
    : GOTO 50
60 GOTO 1
```

Curve Fit—Multiple Linear Regression

This program computes an equation of the form "Z=A+BX+CY" by the least squares method for a given set of three dimensional points (X,Y,Z).

Example: Compute an equation that most closely relates the following data by an equation of the form Z=A+BX+CY.

X	1	2	3
Y	1	2	1
Z	1	0	5

Display	You Enter
>>>	MLR
BEEP	
X?	1
Y?	1
Z?	1
BEEP	
X?	2
Y?	2
Z?	0
BEEP	
X?	3
Y?	1
Z?	5
BEEP	
X?	ENTER
Z=A+BX+CY	ENTER
A= 2.	ENTER
B= 2.	ENTER
C= −3.	ENTER
>>>	

Program length is 270 steps.

LISTING

```
10 "MLR"CLEAR
   : GOTO 30
20 D=D+Y
   : E=E+YY
```

```
   : F=F+XY
   : G=G+Z
   : H=H+XZ
   : I=I+YZ
30 BEEP 1
   : INPUT"X?",X,"Y?",Y,"Z?",Z
   : A=A+1
   : B=B+X
   : C=C+XX
   : GOTO 20
40 M=(AC-BB)*(AI-DG)
   : N=(AF-BD)*(AH-BG)
50 L=(M-N) / ((AC-BB)*(AE-DD)-(AF-BD)^2)
60 K=(AH-BG-L*(AF-BD)) / (AC-BB)
   : J=(G-LD-KB) / A
70 PRINT"Z=A+B+CY"
   : PRINT"A= ";J
   : PRINT"B= ";K
   : PRINT"C= ";L
   : GOTO 1
```

Curve Fit—Parabolic

This program uses the least squares method to fit a parabolic equation (Y=A+BX+CX^2) to a set of given X,Y points. Example: Fit a parabolic curve to the following data.

X	0	1	2	3
Y	1.1	3.1	6.9	12.9

Display	You Enter
>>>	CFP
BEEP	
X?	0
Y?	1.1
BEEP	
X?	1
Y?	3.1
BEEP	
X?	2
Y?	6.9
BEEP	
X?	3
Y?	12.9
BEEP	
X?	ENTER
Y=A+BX+CX^2	ENTER
A= 1.12	ENTER
B= 0.92	ENTER
C= 1	ENTER
R^2= .9999010391	ENTER
NEW X?	4
20.8	ENTER
NEW X?	ENTER
>>>	

Program length is 337 steps.

LISTING

```
10 "CFP"CLEAR
   : GOTO 30
20 H=H+XXXX
   : I=I+Y
```

```
    : J=J+XY
    : K=K+XXY
    : L=L+YY
30 BEEP 1
    : INPUT"X?",X,"Y?",Y
    : D=D+1
    : E=E+X
    : F=F+XX
    : G=G+XXX
    : GOTO 20
40 M=DFH+2EGF-FFF-EEH-DGG
    : A=(HFI+EGK+FJG-FFK-EJH-IGG) / M
50 B=(DJH+IGF+FEK-FJF-IEH-DGK) / M
    :C=(DFK+EJF+IEG-FFI-EEK-DJG) / M
60 R=(AI+BJ+CK-II / D) / (L-II / D)
    : PRINT"Y=A+BX+CX^2"
70 PRINT"A= ";A
    : PRINT"B= ";B
    : PRINT"C= ";C
    : PRINT"R^2= ";R
80 INPUT"NEW X?",X
    : PRINT A+BX+CXX
    : GOTO 80
90 GOTO 1
```

Decimal to Fraction Conversion

This program computes successively more accurate fractions as approximations to a decimal number X.
For example: Approximate the value of PI with fractions.

Display	You Enter
>>>	DF
?	π
3. / 1.	ENTER
ERR= −0.141592654	ENTER
22. / 7.	ENTER
ERR= 1.26448885 E−03	ENTER
333. / 106.	ENTER
ERR= −8.322004 E−05	ENTER
355. / 113.	ENTER
ERR= 2.6635 E−07	ENTER
(etc.)	

Program length is 130 steps.

LISTING

```
10 "DF"INPUT X
   : A=INT X
   : B=1
   : C=X-A
   : D=0
   : E=1
   : F=1
   : G=0
20 H=AF+D
   : I=AG+E
   : Y=H / I-X
   : PRINT H;" / ";I
   : PRINT"ERR = ";Y
30 A=INT (B / C)
   : J=C
   : C=B-AC
   : B=J
   : D=F
   : F=H
```

```
: E=G
: G=I
: GOTO 20
```

Derivatives of a Function

This collection of three programs computes the 0th, 1st, and 2nd derivatives of a user defined function "FX". The 0th derivative is just the function itself, the 1st derivative is the slope of the function, and the 2nd derivative relates to the curvature. A small delta increment of .0001 may optionally be altered when asked for D?

Example: Analyze the function $Y=X^3$ at X=1. First, verify that the function FX has been programmed as in line 900.

Display	You Enter
>>>	D0
X?	1
F (X) = 1.	ENTER
>>>	D1
X?	1
D?	ENTER
DX= 3.000005	ENTER
>>>	D2
X?	1
D?	ENTER
DDX= 6.	ENTER
>>>	

Program length is 231 steps.

LISTING

```
10 "D0"INPUT"X?",X
   : GOSUB"FX"
   : PRINT"F(X)= ";Y
   : GOTO 1
20 "D1"D=E-4
   : INPUT"X?",W,"D?",D
30 FOR E=1 TO 2
   : X=W+DE-3D / 2
   : GOSUB"FX"
   : A(E)=Y
   : NEXT E
```

```
 40 Z=(B−A) / D
    : PRINT"DX= ";Z
    : GOTO 1
 50 "D2"D=E−4
    : INPUT"X?",W,"D?",D
 60 FOR E=1 TO 3
    : X=W+DE−2D
    : GOSUB"FX"
    : A(E)=Y
    : NEXT E
 70 Z=(A+C−2B) / DD
    : PRINT"DDX= ";Z
    : GOTO 1
900 "FX"Y=XXX
    :RETURN
```

Determinant—Two by Two Matrix

This program computes the determinant of a four element square matrix (2 by 2). For example, compute the determinant of the following matrix.

$$\begin{matrix} 1 & 2 \\ 3 & -4 \end{matrix}$$

Display	You Enter
>>>	DT2
?	1
?	2
?	3
?	−4
−10.	ENTER
>>>	

Program length is 26 steps.

LISTING

```
10 "DT2"INPUT A,B,C,D
   : PRINT AD-BC
   : GOTO 1
```

Determinant—
Three by Three Matrix

This program computes the determinant of a nine element square matrix (3 by 3). For example, compute the determinant of the following matrix.

1	2	3
1.2	0	−1
−2	4	2.7

Display	You Enter
>>>	DT3
?	1
?	2
?	3
?	1.2
?	0
?	−1
?	−2
?	4
?	2.7
15.92	ENTER
>>>	

Program length is 54 steps.

LISTING

```
10 "DT3"INPUT A,B,C,D,E,F,G,H,I
   : PRINT AEI+BFG+CDH−CEG−BDI−AFH
   : GOTO 1
```

Dice Thrower

This program rolls a pair of pseudorandom dice. Use the ON / BREAK key to terminate the program.

Display	You Enter
> > >	DICE
2.1.	ENTER
2.5.	ENTER
1.4.	ENTER
1.1.	ENTER
6.3.	ENTER
4.2.	ON / BREAK
BREAK AT 10	

Program length is 62 steps.

LISTING

```
10 "DICE"GOSUB"R"
   : A=1+INT 6R
   : GOSUB"R"
   : PRINT 1+INT 6R;A
   : GOTO 10
20 "R"R= π +983R
   : R=R-INT R
   : RETURN
```

Differential Equations

This program computes a numerical solution for differential equations by the Runge-Kutta method. The differential equation should be in the form Y'=f(X,Y). FX is the label to use where you program your equation. Use Z in place of Y' as the return variable. Example: Compute a solution to Y'=X+Y given initial conditions of X=0 and Y=0. Use an increment of .5.

Display		You Enter
>>>		DE
X0?		0
Y0?		0
INC?		.5
0.5	0.1484375	ENTER
1.	0.717346	ENTER
1.5	1.979375363	ENTER
2.	4.383970325	ENTER
2.5	8.672013583	ENTER
(etc.)		

Program length is 171 steps.

LISTING

```
10 "DE"INPUT"X0?",V,"Y0",W,"INC?",I
20 X=V
   : Y=W
   : GOSUB"FX"
   : A=IZ
   : X=V+I / 2
   : Y=W+A / 2
   : GOSUB"FX"
   : B=IZ
   : Y=W+B / 2
   : GOSUB"FX"
30 C=IZ
   : X=V+I
   : Y=W+C
   : GOSUB:"FX"
   : D=IZ
   : V=V+I
```

```
   : W=W+(A+2B+2C+D) / 6
   : PRINT V,W
   : GOTO 20
900 "FX"Z=X+Y
   : RETURN
```

Distribution—Binomial

This program computes the binomial distribution function given X, n, and p.

$$b(X;n,p) = \frac{n!}{X!\,(n-X)!}\ p^{x}\,(1-p)^{n-x}$$

Example: Compute the binomial distribution function for X=9, n=10, and p=.8.

Display	You Enter
>>>	BIN
X?	9
N?	10
P?	.8
.268435456	ENTER
>>>	

Program length is 115 steps.

LISTING

```
10 "BIN"INPUT"X?",X,"N?",N,"P?",P
20 A=N
   : B=X
   : C=A
   : IF A-B > B LET B=A-B
30 FOR Z=1 TO B
   : C=C / Z
   : IF A-Z > A-B LET C=CA-CZ
40 NEXT Z
   : PRINT P^X*(1-P)^(N-X)*C
   : GOTO 1
```

Distribution—Hypergeometric

This program computes the hypergeometric distribution function given X, sample size n, population or lot size N, and "successes" in the population a.

$$h(X;n,a,N) = \frac{\binom{a}{x}\binom{N-a}{n-X}}{\binom{N}{n}}$$

For example, what is the probability of obtaining 2 defectives in a sample of size 8 taken without replacement from a population of 30 items containing 7 defectives?

Display	You Enter
>>>	HYP
X?	2
SAMP SIZE?	8
SUCCESSES?	7
LOT SIZE?	30
.3621927498	ENTER
>>>	

Program length is 176 steps.

LISTING

```
10 "HYP"INPUT"X?",X,"SAMP SIZE?",N,"SUCCESSES?",
   S,"LOT SIZE?",L
20 A=S
  : B=X
  : GOSUB 30
  : V=C
  : A=L-S
  : B=N-X
  : GOSUB 30
  : W=C
  : A=L
  : B=N
  : GOSUB 30
  : PRINT VW / C
  : GOTO 1
30 C=A
  : IF A-B > B LET B=A-B
```

```
40 FOR Z=1 TO B
   : C=C / Z
   : IF A-Z > A-B LET C=CA-CZ
50 NEXT Z
   : RETURN
```

Distribution—Normal

This program computes the normal distribution function of X. Example: Compute the normal distribution function if X = 1.23.

Display	You Enter
>>>	NORM
X?	1.23
N= .8906513833	ENTER
>>>	

Program length is 146 steps.

LISTING

```
10 'NORM"INPUT"X?",X
   : T=1 / (1+.2316419X)
   : U=EXP (-XX / 2) / √2 π
   : V=TTT
20 N=.31938153T-.356563782TT
   +1.781477937V-1.821255978TV+1.330274429TTV
30 N=1-UN
   : PRINT "N= ";N
   : GOTO 1
```

Distribution—Poisson

This program computes the Poisson distribution given X and lambda.

$$\text{Poisson}(X;\lambda) = \frac{e^{-\lambda}\lambda^{x}}{X!}$$

For example, compute the Poisson distribution function if X = 2 and lambda = 3. 4.

Display	You Enter
>>>	POI
X?	2
LAMBDA?	3. 4
.1928975004	ENTER
>>>	

Program length is 62 steps.

LISTING

```
10 "POI"INPUT"X?"X,"LAMBDA?",L
20 F=1
   : FOR Z=1 TO X
   : F=FZ
   : NEXT Z
   : PRINT EXP-L*L^X / F
   : GOTO 1
```

Electronics—Balanced Bridge

This program computes the complex impedance for one leg of a balanced bridge given the other three. (Fig. 10) The second impedance to be entered is opposite the unknown. For instance, given Z1=3+4j, Z2=5, and Z3=5j compute Z4.

Display	You Enter
>>>	BRI
R1?	3
I1?	4
R2?	5
I2?	0
R3?	0
I3?	5
−4. 3.	ENTER
>>>	

Or, Z4 = −4+3j.

Program length is 116 steps.

LISTING

```
10 "BRI"INPUT"R1?",A,"I1?",
   B,"R2?",C,"I2?",D,"R3?",E,"I3?",F
20 I=AE−BF
   : J=AF+BE
   : K=CC+DD
   : G=(IC+JD) / K
   : H=(JC−ID) / K
30 PRINT G,H
   : GOTO 1
```

Balanced Bridge

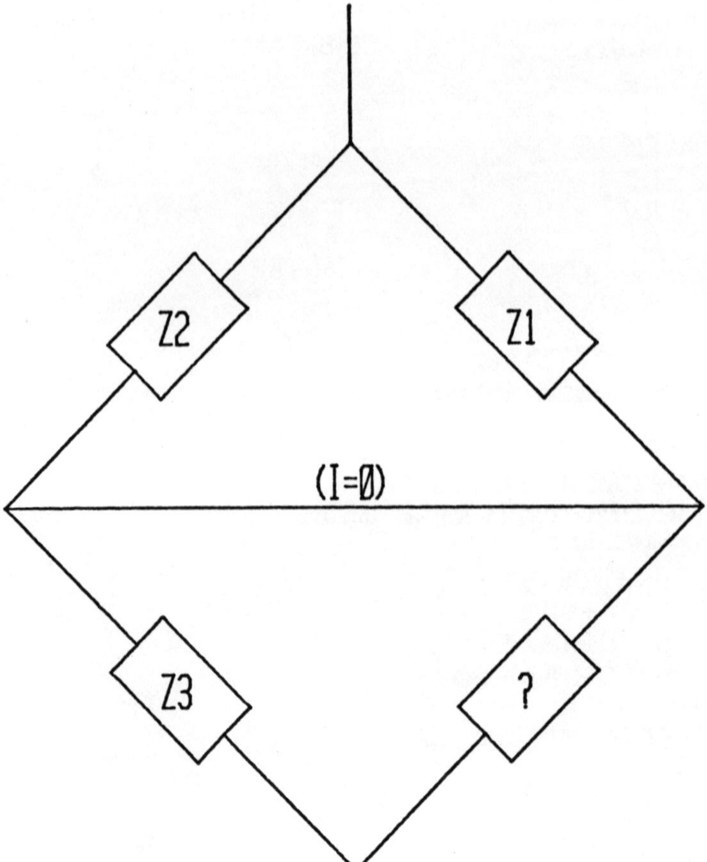

Fig. 10.

Electronics—Decibels

This program provides conversions between power, voltage, or current ratios and decibels. When asked to input an unknown value, just press ENTER.

DB = 10 * LOG(Power ratio)
DB = 20 * LOG(Voltage or Current ratio)

Example: Convert a voltage ratio of 2 to decibels, then convert −3 decibels to a power ratio.

Display	You Enter
> > >	DCBL
DB?	ENTER
I OR E RATIO?	2
DB= 6.020*E*00	ENTER
I OR E RATIO= 2.000*E*00	ENTER
POWER RATIO= 4.000*E*00	ENTER
> > >	DCBL
DB?	−3
DB= −3.000*E*00	ENTER
I OR E RATIO= 7.079*E*01	ENTER
POWERRATIO=5.011*E*−01	ENTER
> > >	

Program length is 165 steps.

LISTING

```
10 "DCBL"INPUT"DB?",D
   : GOTO 40
20 INPUT"I OR E RATIO?",A
   : D=20*LOG A
   : GOTO 40
30 INPUT"POWER RATIO?",B
   : D=10*LOG B
40 B=10^.1D
   : A=10^.05D
   : USING".# # #^"
50 PRINT"DB= ";D
   : PRINT"I OR E RATIO=";A
   : PRINT"POWER RATIO= ";B
   : GOTO 1
```

Electronics—Ohm's Law

This program flexibly computes answers to problems involving voltage, current, resistance, and power. You input any two values and the other two will be computed. Just ENTER when asked for the unknown values. All solutions are derived from two equations.

$$E = I*R \text{ and } P = I*E$$

For instance, at what voltage will a 2 ohm resistor use 18 watts of power? What current will it be drawing?

Display	You Enter
>>>	OHM
P?	18
I?	ENTER
E?	ENTER
R?	2
P= 18.	ENTER
I= 3.	ENTER
E= 6.	ENTER
R= 2.	ENTER
>>>	

Program length is 178 steps.

LISTING

```
 10 "OHM"CLEAR
    : INPUT"P?",P
 20 INPUT"I?",I
 30 INPUT"E?",E
 40 INPUT"R?",R
 50 IF PI LET E=P / I
 60 IF PE LET I=P / E
 70 IF PR LET I= √(P / R)
 80 IF IE LET R=E / I
 90 IF IR LET P=IIR
100 IF ER LET I=E / R
110 IF PIER=0 THEN 50
120 PRINT"P= ";P
    : PRINT"I= ";I
```

```
130 PRINT"E= ";E
    : PRINT"R= ";R
    : GOTO 1
```

Electronics—RC Timing

This program solves for any one of six variables given the other five. They all relate to the charging curve of a resistor and capacitor following a voltage step. (Fig. 11)

Just press ENTER when asked for the unknown. Don't enter zero for a known value. Use a small number such as E −99.

All solutions are derived from the same equation.

$$Vi = (V_1 - V_2)\, e^{\frac{-t}{RC}} + V_2$$

Example: A 47 microfarad capacitor and a .1 megohm resistor are in series. How long will it take for the capacitor to change up to 4.3 volts after 5 volts is applied?

Display	You Enter
>>>	RC
V1?	E −99
V2?	5
VI?	4.3
R?	.1E6
C?	47E−6
T?	ENTER
9.240730423 =T	ENTER
>>>	

The answer is approximately 9.24 seconds.
Program length is 239 steps.

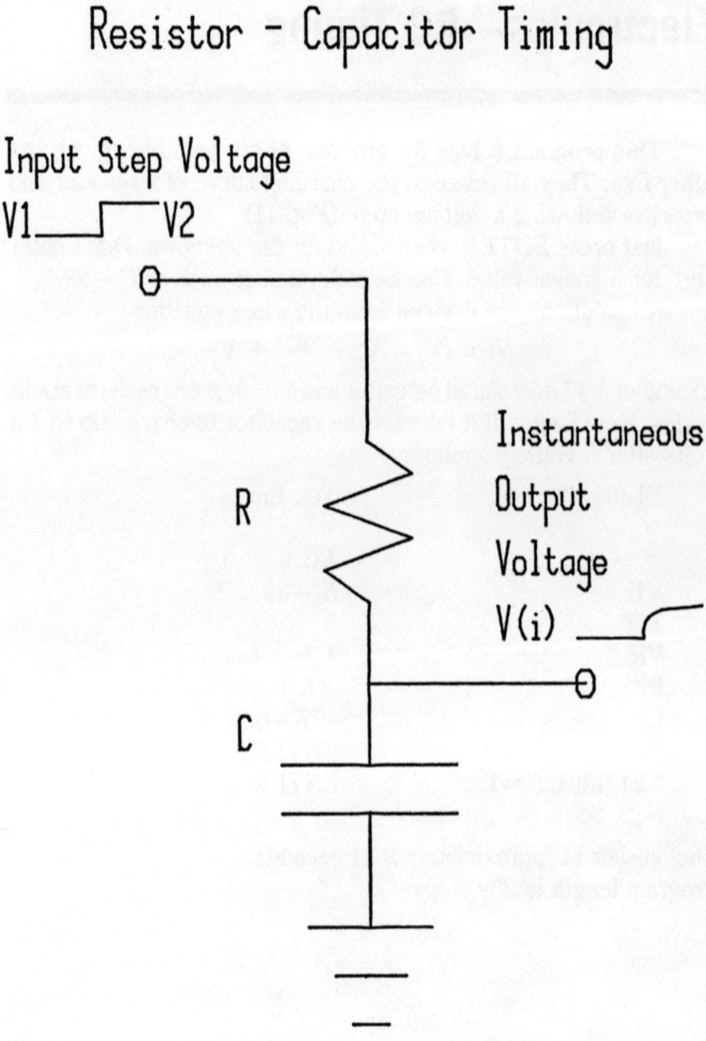

Resistor - Capacitor Timing
Input Step Voltage
V1
V2
R
Instantaneous
Output
Voltage
V(i)
C

Fig. 11.

LISTING

```
 10 "RC"CLEAR
    : INPUT"V1?",V
 20 INPUT"V2?",W
 30 INPUT"VI?",X
 40 INPUT"R?",R
 50 INPUT"C?",C
 60 INPUT"T?",T
 70 B=-LN((W-X) / (W-V))
    : IF ABS RC LET A=EXP (-T / R / C)
 80 IF V=0 PRINT W-W / A+X / A;" =V1"
 90 IF W=0 PRINT (X-AV) / (1-A); " =V2"
100 IF X=0 PRINT W-AW+AV;" =VI"
110 IF R=0 PRINT T / B / C;" =R"
120 IF C=0 PRINT T / B / R;" =C"
130 IF T=0 PRINT BRC;" = T"
140 GOTO 1
```

Electronics—Resistor Analysis

This pair of programs computes equivalent resistances for four configurations of resistors. (Fig. 12)

RR—If you have two resistors in either a parallel or series configuration. The answer on the left is the equivalent for parallel resistors, on the right for series.

RRR—If you have three resistors in either a delta or wye configuration. The answers on the left are delta equivalents of the wye resistor in an opposite position. The answers on the right are wye equivalents of the delta resistor in an opposite position.

First example: Compute the equivalent resistance of 200 ohm and 300 ohm resistors in parallel.

Display	You Enter
>>>	RR
?	200
?	300
120. 500.	ENTER (Answer is 120 ohms.)
>>>	

Second example: Compute the wye network equivalant of a delta configuration composed of 500 ohm, 700 ohm, and 800 ohm resistors.

Display		You Enter
>>>		RRR
?		500
?		700
?		800
TO DELTA,	TO WYE	ENTER (Answers will be on right.)
2620.	280.	ENTER
1871.428571	200.	ENTER
1637.5	175.	ENTER
>>>		

Or, referring to the bottom of figure:

$R_A = 500$ $R_1 = 280$
$R_B = 700$ $R_2 = 200$
$R_C = 800$ $R_3 = 175$

Program length is 142 steps.

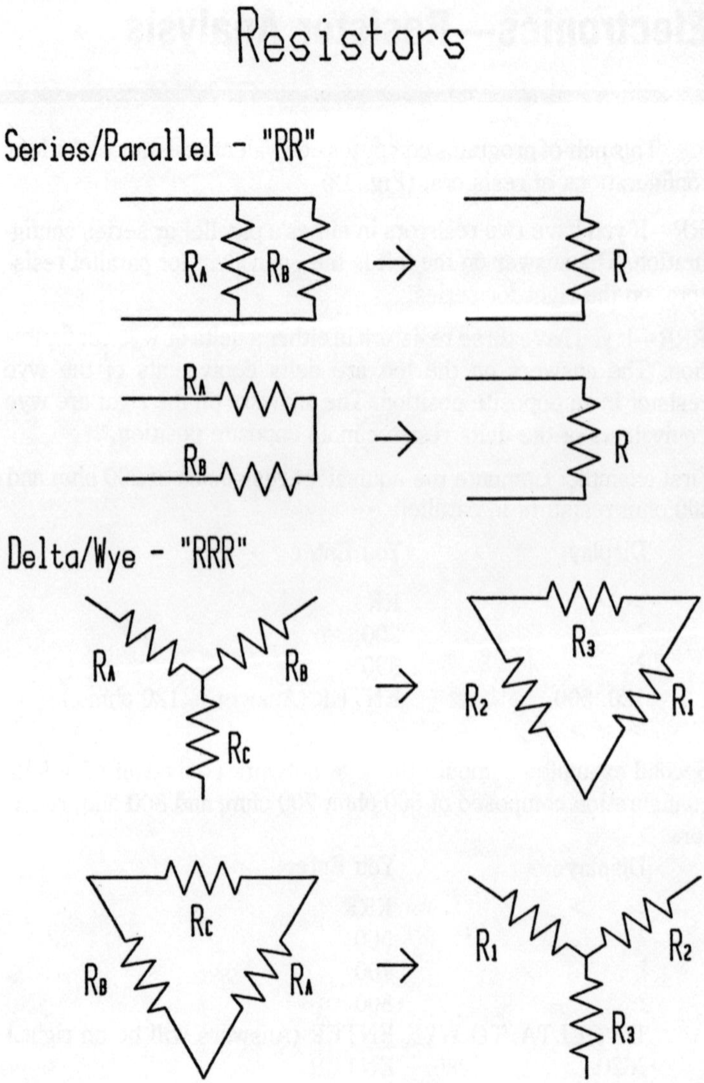
Resistors
Series/Parallel - "RR"
RA
RB
R
RA
RB
R
Delta/Wye - "RRR"
RA
RB
RC
R3
R2
R1
RC
RB
RA
R1
R2
R3

Fig. 12.

LISTING

```
10 "RR"INPUT A,B
   : C=A+B
   : PRINT AB / C,C
   : GOTO 1
20 "RRR"INPUT A,B,C
   : J=A+B+C
   : K=AB+BC+CA
30 D=K / A
   : E=K / B
   : F=K / C
   : G=BC / J
   : H=AC / J
   : I=AB / J
40 PRINT"TO DELTA, TO WYE"
   : PRINT D,G
   : PRINT E, H
   : PRINT F, I
   : GOTO 1
```

Electronics—Resonant Frequency

This program computes values at resonant frequency for inductance, capacitance, and frequency. You enter any two values and the third is computed. Also computed is the reactance at resonance. (Fig. 13) Input a value of 0 for the unknown.

$$F = \frac{1}{2\pi\sqrt{LC}}$$

$$X = 2\pi FL$$

Example: Compute the resonant frequency for an inductance of 88 millihenry and a capacitance of 1 microfarad in a parallel tank circuit. What is the reactance of the inductor at this frequency?

Display	You Enter
>>>	FLC
F?	0
L?	.088
C?	*E* –6
F= 536.5112037	ENTER
X= 296.6479395	ENTER
>>>	

Program length is 133 steps.

LISTING

```
10 "FLC"INPUT"F?",F,"L?",L,"C?",C
20 IF F=0 LET F=1 / (2 π * √LC)
   : PRINT"F= ";F
30 IF L=0 LET L=1 / 4 π π FFC
   : PRINT"L= ";L
40 IF C=0 LET C=1 /4 π π FFL
   : PRINT"C= ";C
50 X=2 π FL
   : PRINT"X= ";X
   : GOTO 1
```

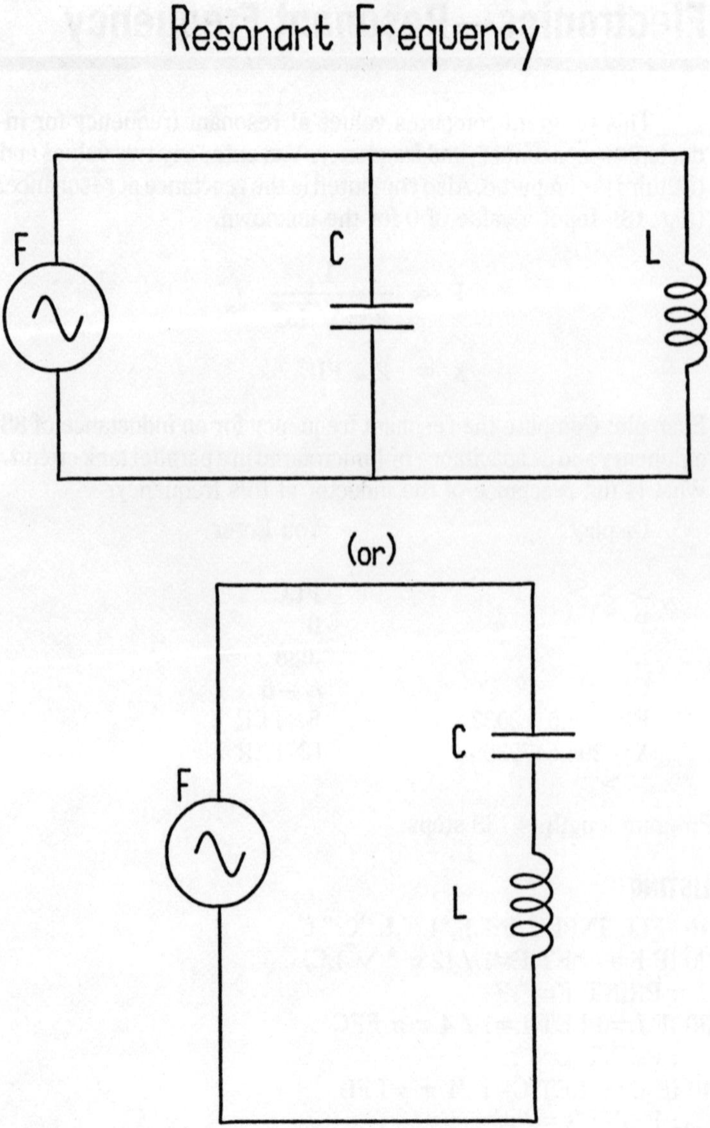

Fig. 13.

Error Function—And Complement

This program computes the error function of X and its complement. The computations are iterative and may be continued until the desired accuracy is achieved. For example: Compute erf (3.7) and cerf (3.7).

Display	You Enter
>>>	ERF
X?	3.7
ITERATIVE APPROXIMATION	
ERF– > 9.999998334 $E-01$	ENTER
CERF– > 1.665609656 $E-07$	ENTER
ITERATIVE APPROXIMATION	
ERF– > 9.999998328 $E-01$	ENTER
CERF– > 1.672527747 $E-07$	ENTER
ITERATIVE APPROXIMATION	
ERF– > 9.999998329 $E-01$	ENTER
CERF– > 1.6712644 $E-07$	ENTER
(etc.)	

Program length is 224 steps.

LISTING

```
10 "ERF"INPUT"X?",X
   : A=2*EXP -XX / √π
   : B=A / 2X
   : G=X > 3
   : S=G
   : N=G
   : F=G
20 M=2N+1-2G
   : F=2*(F=-1)-1
   : W=1
   : FOR Z=1 TO M STEP 2
   : W=WZ
   : NEXT Z
30 IF G LET S=S+FW / (2XX)^N
   : C=BS
   : E=1-C
   : GOTO 50
```

```
40 S=S+2^N*X^M / W
   : E=AS
   : C=1–E
50 PAUSE"ITERATIVE APPROXIMATION"
   : PRINT"ERF– > ";E
   : PRINT"CERF– > ";C
   : N=N+1
   : GOTO 20
```

Euler Function

This program computes the Euler function of a positive integer. The Euler function is the number of integers not exeeding and relatively prime to N. Example: Compute the Euler function of 34 and 35.

Display	You Enter
> > >	EU
?	34
16.	ENTER
> > >	EU
?	35
24.	ENTER
> > >	

Program length is 103 steps.

LISTING

```
10 "EU"INPUT N
   : A=1
   : B=2
   : C=1
20 D=N / B
   : E=INT D
   : IF B > D PRINT AN-A*(N < > C)
   : GOTO 1
30 IF D > E LET B=B+2-(B=2)
   : GOTO 20
40 N=D
   : A=AB-A*(B < > C)
   : C=B
   : GOTO 20
```

Euler Numbers

This program computes the Nth Euler number. For example: Compute the 5th Euler number.

Display	You Enter
> > >	EN
?	5
EULER = 50521.	ENTER
> > >	

Program length is 74 steps.

LISTING

```
10 "EN"INPUT N
   : D=2N
   : F=1
   : FOR Z=2 TO D
   : F=FZ
   : NEXT Z
20 E=INT(F*2^(D+2) /π^ (D+1)
   : PRINT"EULER= ";E
   : GOTO 1
```

EXP(X) for Large X

This program computes EXP(X) for X that would normally cause a numerical overflow. For instance: Compute EXP(1) and EXP(9999).

Display	You Enter
>>>	EX
?	1
2.718281828 E0.	ENTER
>>>	EX
?	9999
3.23985072 E4342.	ENTER
>>>	

Program length is 47 steps.

LISTING

```
10 "EX"INPUT X
   : B=X / LN 10
   : A=10^(B-INT B)
   : B=INT B
   : PRINT A;" E";B
   : GOTO 1
```

EXP(X) for Large X

Factorial—Three Versions

This collection of three programs demonstrates several approaches to computing the factorial of an integer.

$$X! = X*(X-1)*(X-2)*(X-3)* \ldots *3*2*1$$

FA1—The integers 1 through X are multiplied together. This method is great for smaller values of X.
FA2—Here, we sum the logarithms of the integers 1 through X. This allows us to compute large factorials that would normally overflow our number range. This approach is time consuming for large values of X.
FA3—This is Stirling's formula, an approximation that is faster for large values of X. Accuracy is best for larger X values.

$$X! \cong \sqrt{(2 \pi X)} X^x e^{-x}$$

Example: Compute 9! using each program.

Display	You Enter
>>>	FA1
?	9
362880.	ENTER
>>>	FA2
?	9
3.628799993 E5.	ENTER
>>>	FA3
?	9
359536.8728	ENTER
>>>	

Program length is 117 steps.

LISTING

```
10 "FA1"INPUT X
  : Y=1
  : FOR Z=1 TO X
  : Y=YZ
  : NEXT Z
  : PRINT Y
  : GOTO 1
20 "FA2"INPUT X
  : Y=0
```

```
     : FOR Z=1 TO X
     : Y=Y+LOG Z
     : NEXT Z
     : Z=INT Y
     : PRINT 10^(Y−Z);" E";Z
     : GOTO 1
30 "FA3"INPUT X
     : PRINT √2 πX*X^X / EXP X
     : GOTO 1
```

Factors of a Positive Integer

This program computes the prime factors of a positive integer. For instance: Compute the factors of 140.

Display	You Enter
>>>	FS
?	140
2.	ENTER
2.	ENTER
5.	ENTER
7.	ENTER
BEEP	
>>>	

Or, 2*2*5*7 = 140.
Program length is 71 steps.

LISTING

```
10 "FS"INPUT X
   : Y=1
20 Y=Y+1
   : IF Y > √X THEN 50
30 Z=X / Y
   : IF INT Z=Z PRINT Y
   : X=Z
   : Y=1
40 GOTO 20
50 PRINT X
   : BEEP 1
   : GOTO 1
```

Fibonacci Numbers

This program generates a Fibonacci number sequence. Each term is the sum of the previous two terms. You choose the first two terms.

Display	You Enter
> > >	F1B
F1?	0
F2?	1
1. 0.	ENTER
2. 1.	ENTER
3. 1.	ENTER
4. 2.	ENTER
5. 3.	ENTER
6. 5.	ENTER
7. 8.	ENTER
8. 13.	ENTER
9. 21.	ENTER
10. 34.	ENTER
(etc.)	

Program length is 57 steps.

LISTING

```
10 "FIB"CLEAR
   : INPUT"F1?",A,"F2?",B
20 N=N+1
   : PRINT N,A
   : C=A+B
   : A=B
   : B=C
   : GOTO 20
```

Flash Cards—Multiplication Table

This program makes learning the multiplication table fun! A sequence of twenty multiplication problems is presented. The correct answer is shown if an incorrect response is entered. Afterwards, your percent score is displayed.

The difficulty of the set of problems is controlled by responding to the LARGEST NUMBER? Question. Answering 10 will produce random problems up to 10 * 10. For a greater challenge you might consider a LARGEST NUMBER of 100 or 1000.

Each multiplication problem is shown temporarily before you're prompted with a "?". To review the problem, just press ENTER.

Display	You Enter
>>>	MT
LARGEST NUMBER?	10
8. * 5.	
?	40
YES ! ! !	
2. * 8.	
?	ENTER
2. * 8.	
?	17
BEEP, BEEP, BEEP	
2. * 8. =16.!!!	
2. * 8. =16.!!!	
2. * 8. =16.!!!	
2. * 8. =16.!!!	
2. * 8. =16.!!!	
6. * 10.	
?	60
YES ! ! !	
(After twenty problems . . .)	
BEEP, BEEP, BEEP, BEEP, BEEP	
YOUR SCORE IS 85%	ENTER
>>>	

Program length is 227 steps.

LISTING

```
10 "MT"H=0
   : N=10
   : INPUT"LARGEST NUMBER?",N
20 FOR Z=1 TO 20
   : GOSUB 80
   : A=B
   : GOSUB 80
30 PAUSE A;" * ";B
   : INPUT Q
   : GOTO 50
40 GOTO 30
50 IF Q=AB PAUSE" YES ! ! !"
   : H=H+1
   : GOTO 70
60 BEEP 3
   : C=AB
   : FOR Y=1 TO 5
   : PAUSE A;"*";B;"=";C;"! ! !"
   : NEXT Y
70 NEXT Z
   : S=5H
   : BEEP 5
   : PRINT"YOUR SCORE IS ";S;"%"
   : GOTO 1
80 R= π + 997R
   : R=R-INT R
   : B=1 + INT (N-RRN)
   : RETURN
```

Fractions

This program does simple math with fractions. The answers are expressed as a fraction reduced to its lowest terms. There are five programs available.

F+	N1 / D1 + N2 / D2
F–	N1 / D1 – N2 / D2
F*	N1 / D1 * N2 / D2
F /	N1 / D1 / N2 / D2
FLT	Reduces N / D to lowest terms.

Answers are returned in variables A and B. So, to chain several computations, enter A and B when asked for "N1?" and "D1?". An example for each program will help clarify their use.

F+ What is 7 / 12 + 2 / 3?

Display	You Enter
>>>	F+
N1?	7
D1?	12
N2?	2
D2?	3
5. / 4.	ENTER
>>>	

Answer is 5 / 5.

F–What is 7 / 12 – 2 / 3 + 5 / 6 ? This example will also demonstrate how to chain computations.

Display	You Enter	
>>>	F –	
N1?	7	
D1?	12	
N2?	2	
D2?	3	
–1. / 12.	ENTER	(This is 7 / 12 – 2 / 3)
>>>	F+	
N1?	A	
D1?	B	
N2?	5	
D2?	6	
3. / 4.	ENTER	
>>>		

Answer is 3 / 4.
What is 2 / 3 * 7 / 16?

Display	You Enter
> > >	F*
N1?	2
D1?	3
N2?	7
D2?	16
7. / 24.	ENTER
> > >	

Answer is 7 / 24.
F / What is 7 / 24 / 7 / 16?

Display	You Enter
> > >	F /
N1?	7
D1?	24
N2?	7
D2?	16
2. / 3.	ENTER
> > >	

Answer is 2 / 3.
FLT Reduce 171 / 399 to lowest terms.

Display	You Enter
> > >	FLT
N?	171
D?	399
3. / 7.	ENTER
> > >	

Answer is 3 / 7.
Program length is 232 steps.

LISTING

```
 10 "F+"GOSUB 50
    : A=AD+BC
    : B=BD
    : GOTO 90
 20 "F-"GOSUB 50
    : A=AD-BC
    : B=BD
    : GOTO 90
 30 "F*"GOSUB 50
    : A=AC
    : B=BD
    : GOTO 90
 40 "F / "GOSUB 50
    : A=AD
    : B=BC
    : GOTO 90
 50 INPUT"N1?",A,"D1?",B
 60 INPUT"N2?",C,"D2?",D
 70 RETURN
 80 "FLT"INPUT"N?",A,"D?",B
 90 X=A
    : Y=B
100 Z=X-Y*INT(X / Y)
    : X=Y
    : Y=Z
    : IF Z THEN 100
110 A=A / X
    : B=B / X
    : PRINT A;" / ";B
    : GOTO 1
```

Games—"Deal 'Em"

This program shuffles and deals a deck of cards without repeating any cards. The cards may be shuffled at any time by restarting the program. Or, if all the cards have been dealt, the program will automatically reshuffle the deck. The deck comes complete with two jokers.

Display	You Enter
>>>	DEAL
BEEP	
SHUFFLING	
8 OF CLUBS	ENTER
7 OF SPADES	ENTER
QUEEN OF HEARTS	ENTER
(etc.)	

Program length is 357 steps. Also required are 54 variables in flexible memory.

LISTING

```
10 "DEAL"BEEP 1
   : PAUSE"SHUFFLING"
   : FOR Z=27 TO 80
   : A(Z)=0
   : NEXT Z
20 Y=0
   : R= π + 997R
   : R=R-INT R
   : Z=27+INT 54R
30 Y=Y+1
   : IF Y=55 THEN 10
40 Z=Z+7
   : Z=Z-54*(Z>80)
   : IF A(Z) THEN 30
45 A(Z)=1
   : IF Z > 78 PRINT"JOKER"
   : GOTO 20
50 E$="HEARTS"
   : IF Z > 39 LET E$="SPADES"
   : IF Z > 52 LET E$="CLUBS"
   : IF Z > 65 LET E$="DIAMOND"
```

```
60 Z=Z-13*INT( (Z-1) / 13)
   : IF Z=1 PRINT"ACE OF ";E$
   : GOTO 20
70 IF Z < 11 PRINT USING "# # #";Z;" OF ";E$
   : GOTO 20
80 X$="JACK"
   : IF Z > 11 LET X$="QUEEN"
   : IF Z > 12 LET X$="KING"
90 PRINT X$," OF ";E$
   : GOTO 20
```

Games—"Huh?"

How's your short term memory? This program might help develop your memory, but then again it just might drive you crazy!

The rules are simple. You'll be shown a number and then be asked to repeat it. It starts easy, with a one digit number, but for every correct guess the number of digits increases by one. When you guess incorrectly the number shrinks by one digit, so don't panic! After about a dozen numbers your score will be displayed.

Display	You Enter
>>>	HUH
1	
YOUR GUESS?	1
YES!	
32	
YOUR GUESS?	32
YES!	

. . . (After several more numbers) . . .

Display	You Enter
50247	
YOUR GUESS?	52674
NO!	
2319	
YOUR GUESS?	2319
YES!	
BEEP, BEEP, BEEP	
YOUR SCORE= 52.27%	ENTER
>>>	

Program length is 266 steps.

LISTING

```
10 "HUH"H=0
   : L=1
   : Q=0
   : Z=0
20 L=10L*(L< E10)+L*(L>E9)
   : R= π +983R
   : R=R-INT R
```

```
   : T= π + 977T
   : T=T−INT T
30 N=INT(LR + LT / 997)
   : N=N+(N=0)
   : PAUSE N
40 J=INT LOG 10N
   : INPUT"YOUR GUESS?",G
   : IF G=N PAUSE"YES!"
   : GOTO 60
50 PAUSE"NO!"
   : L=L / (1+99*(L> 1))
   : H=H−J
60 H=H+J
   : Z=Z+J
   : Q=Q+1
   : IF Q < 13 THEN 20
70 BEEP 3
   : S=100H / Z
   : USING"# # # # . # #"
80 PRINT"YOUR SCORE= ";S;"%"
   : GOTO 1
```

Games—"Lunar Landing"

Landing on the moon in one piece has been a popular challenge on larger computers for several years. This program simulates a lunar landing and challenges you to land as softly as possible.

The first few program lines allow you to optionally alter the beginning values for altitude, velocity, and fuel. Just press ENTER for the default values. After you feel confident about your newly acquired lunar landing skills you might try altering your beginning fuel supply. How little fuel is required to accomplish a "NICE!" landing?

With each firing of your retrorockets your current altitude, velocity, and remaining fuel are displayed. To review these values, just press ENTER when asked "USE HOW MUCH FUEL?". Use 0 fuel if you just want to coast awhile.

Several changes and enhancements could be made to this program. You might modify the descriptive terms near the end of the program (the ones relating to landing velocity). Or, try altering the default values if you need more (or less) of a challenge. Also consider testing the rate of fuel use to set a limit.

Display	You Enter
>>>	LUNAR
ALTITUDE?	ENTER (Using default values)
VELOCITY? (–)	ENTER
FUEL?	ENTER
BEEP, BEEP	
HERE WE GO!	
ALTITUDE= 700.	
VELOCITY= –100.	
FUEL LEFT= 100.	
USE HOW MUCH FUEL?	10
ALTITUDE= 606.1084073	
VELOCITY= –87.78318531	
FUEL LEFT= 90.	
USE HOW MUCH FUEL?	

. . . (several firings later)

```
BEEP, BEEP, BEEP, BEEP, BEEP
CRASH, VEL= 36.38548245 ENTER
>>>
```

Program length is 420 steps.

LISTING

```
 10 "LUNAR"X=700
    : V=-100
    : F=-V
 20 INPUT"ALTITUDE?",X
 30 INPUT"VELOCITY? (-)",V
 40 INPUT"FUEL",F
 45 BEEP 2
    : PAUSE"HERE WE GO!"
 50 PAUSE"ALTITUDE= ";X
 60 PAUSE"VELOCITY= ";V
 70 PAUSE"FUEL LEFT = ";F
 80 IF F=0 GOTO 110
 90 BEEP 1
    : INPUT"USE HOW MUCH FUEL?",E
    : GOTO 110
100 GOTO 50
110 IF E > F LET E=F
120 F=F-E
    : A=2.3E-EF / 200-2 π
    : V=V+A
    : X=X+V-A / 2
    : IF X THEN 50
130 BEEP 5
    : V=-V
140 L$="NICE!"
    : IF V > 5 LET L$="OK"
150 IF V > 12 LET L$="BUMPY"
160 IF V > 21 LET L$="CRUNCH"
170 IF V > 29 LET L$="CRASH"
180 IF V > 47 LET L$="SPLASH"
180 IF V > 77 LET L$="CRATER"
200 PRINT L$;", VEL= ";V
    : GOTO 1
```

Games—"Numb"

Your goal is to guess the value of a randomly chosen integer in the range of 1 to 999. With each guess the range narrows, until you finally find it. How many guesses will it take you? To review the range, just press ENTER when asked "YOUR GUESS?".

Display	You Enter
>>>	NUMB
IT FALLS IN THE RANGE OF	
FROM 1 TO 999	
YOUR GUESS?	300
IT FALLS IN THE RANGE OF	
FROM 300 to 999	
YOUR GUESS?	700
... (Several guesses later)	
YOUR GUESS?	473
BEEP, BEEP, BEEP	
NUMBER OF GUESSES= 14	ENTER
>>>	

Program length is 204 steps.

LISTING

```
10 "NUMB"A=1
   : B=999
   : N=0
   : USING"# # # #"
20 R= π + 997R
   : R=R – INT R
   : X=1 + INT BR
30 PAUSE"IT FALLS IN THE RANGE OF"
40 PAUSE"FROM";A;" TO";B
50 INPUT"YOUR GUESS? ";C
   : GOTO 70
60 GOTO 40
70 N=N+1
   : IF C=X BEEP 3
   : PRINT"NUMBER OF GUESSES= ";N
   : GOTO 1
```

```
80 IF C > X LET B=C
   : GOTO 30
90 A=C
   : GOTO 30
```

Games—"Pool"

This program helps you learn to visualize distances and angles, and it's a fun game too. The pool table is a square, 100 units wide and tall. The only pocket is at X,Y = 0,0. For each shot at the pocket you input a distance and angle for your ball to roll. However, normally only bank shots are allowed, as angles greater than 180 or less than −90 degrees are not allowed. (See program line 40). When the ball stops rolling less than 1 unit from 0,0 it's in the pocket. How many shots will it take you?

Display		You Enter
> > >		POOL
X,Y		
72.6894	85.49107	
DISTANCE?		250
ANGLE?		45
X, Y		
49.4660953	62.2677653	
DISTANCE?		187.5
ANGLE?		47.2
X, Y		
23.1386602	0.1578851	
DISTANCE?		23.1
ANGLE?		179.99
BEEP, BEEP, BEEP		
POCKET!		
# SHOTS TAKEN =3.		ENTER
> > >		

Program length is 304 steps.

LISTING

```
10 "POOL"DEGREE
   : S=200
   : N=0
   : GOSUB 200
   : X=SR / 2
   : GOSUB 200
   : Y=SR / 2
   : GOTO 30
```

```
 20 INPUT"DISTANCE?",D,"ANGLE?",A
    : GOTO 40
 30 PAUSE"X,Y"
    : PAUSE X,Y
    : GOTO 20
 40 IF (A < −90) + (A > 180) BEEP 1
    : PAUSE"ILLEGAL ANGLE"
    : GOTO 20
 50 X=X+D*COS A
    : Y=Y+D*SIN A
    : N=N+1
 60 S=200
    : X=X−S*INT(X / S)
    : Y=Y−INT(Y / S)
 70 IF X > S / 2 LET X=S−X
 80 IF Y > S / 2 LET Y=S−Y
 90 IF XX+YY > 1 THEN 30
100 BEEP 3
    : PAUSE"POCKET!"
    : PRINT"# SHOTS TAKEN =";N
    GOTO 1
200 R= π + 997R
    : R=R−INT R
    : RETURN
```

Games—"Wug Hunt"

This is a fairly heavy duty game of logic and deductive analysis. Three WUGS are hiding along a number line from 1 to 99. For each guess you enter two numbers, A and B. If any WUG is hiding exactly behind A or B it is "ZAPPED" and removed from the game. Any WUGS hiding somewhere in the range A to B are TRAPPED, providing a clue as to their hiding spots. Try to ZAP all three in as few guesses as necessary.

Display	You Enter
>>>	WUG
YOUR GUESS A?	25
AND B?	75
YOU TRAPPED 2 OF 3 WUGS	ENTER
YOUR GUESS A?	1
AND B?	24
YOU TRAPPED 0 OF 3 WUGS	ENTER
YOUR GUESS A?	59
AND B?	74
YOU ZAPPED ONE AT 59.	ENTER
YOU TRAPPED 1 OF 2 WUGS	ENTER
. . . (Several guesses later)	
YOUR GUESS A?	81
AND B?	83
YOU ZAPPED ONE AT 83.	ENTER
GUESSES REQUIRED= 12.	ENTER
>>>	

Program length is 287 steps.

LISTING

```
10 "WUG"GOSUB 80
   : X=Z
   : GOSUB 80
   : Y=Z
   : GOSUB 80
   : N=0
20 INPUT"YOUR GUESS A?",A,"AND B?"B
```

```
30 C=0
   : N=N+1
   : FOR I=24 TO 26
   : J=AA(I)+BA(I)-AB-A(I)A(I)
40 IF J=0 PRINT USING;"YOU ZAPPED ONE AT ":A(I)
   : A(I)=0
50 C=C+(J > 0)
   : NEXT I
   : J=SGN X+SGN Y+SGN Z
60 IF J=0 PRINT USING:"GUESSES REQUIRED= ";N
   : GOTO 1
70 PRINT USING"# #";"YOU TRAPPED";C;" OF";J;" WUGS"
   : GOTO 20
80 R= π +983R
   : R=R-INT R
   : Z=INT 99R+1
   : RETURN
```

Gamma Function

This program computes the gamma function of X.

GAMMA(X) = (X−1)!

For instance, compute GAMMA(6.9).

Display	You Enter
>>>	GA
?	6.9
GAMMA= 597.4942476	ENTER
>>>	

Program length is 204 steps.

LISTING

```
10 "GA"INPUT X
   : W=1
   : Y=1
20 IF X > 1 LET X=X-1
   : IF X > 1 LET W=WX
   : GOTO 20
30 A=-.577191652
   : B=.988205891
   : C=-.897056937
   : D=.918206857
40 E=-.756704078
   : F=.482199394
   : G=-.193527818
   : H=.03586343
50 FOR Z=1 TO 8
   : Y=Y+A(Z)*X^Z
   : NEXT Z
   : Q=WY
60 PRINT"GAMMA= ";Q
   : GOTO 1
```

Graphing Helper— Creating a "Nice" Axis

This program automatically scales an axis of a graph. The largest and smallest values to plot, and the number of major divisions on the graph paper are input. A "nice" axis is described that will allow you to produce an efficient graph. For instance: Design a graph if the X values range from −3.4 to 3.27, and the Y values range from 17.7 to 32.7. (Fig. 14) There are 10 divisions for each axis.

Display	You Enter
>>>	GR
SMALLEST VALUE?	−3.4
LARGEST VALUE?	3.27
NUMBER OF DIVS?	10
START AT −4.	ENTER
END AT 6.	ENTER
INCREMENT= 1.	ENTER
>>>	GR
SMALLEST VALUE?	17.7
LARGEST VALUE?	32.7
NUMBER OF DIVS?	10
START AT 16.	ENTER
END AT 36.	ENTER
INCREMENT= 2.	ENTER
>>>	

Program length is 237 steps.

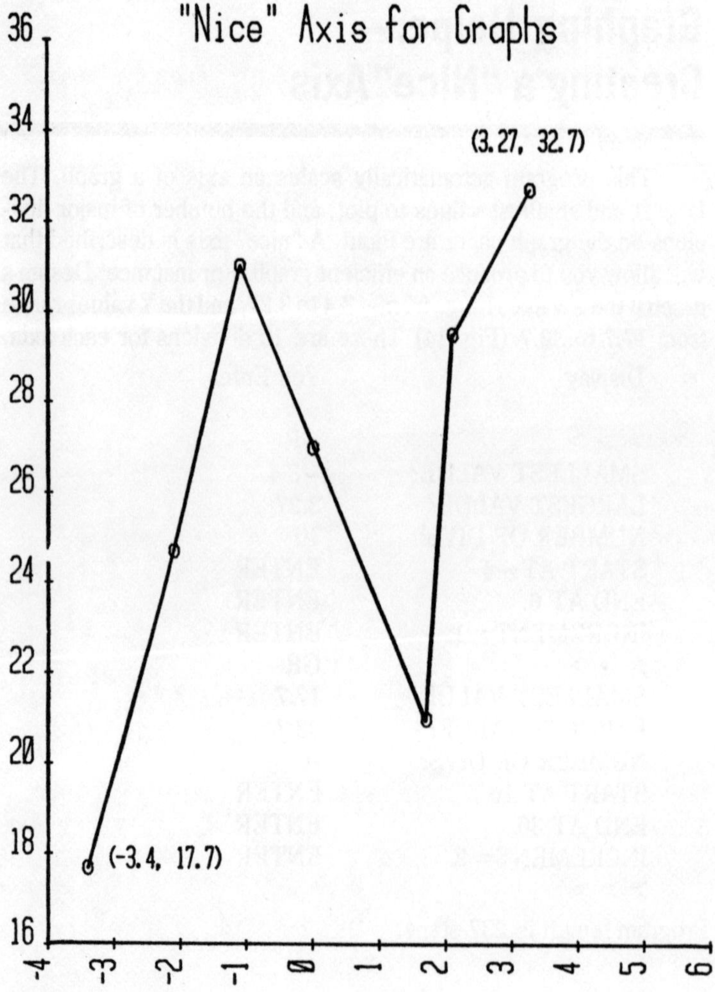
"Nice" Axis for Graphs
36
34
32
30
28
26
24
22
20
18
16
(3.27, 32.7)
(-3.4, 17.7)
-4
-3
-2
-1
0
1
2
3
4
5
6

Fig. 14.

LISTING

```
 10 "GR"INPUT"SMALLEST VAL? ";A
 20 INPUT"LARGEST VAL? ";B
 30 INPUT"NUMBER OF DIVS? ";C
 40 E=1
    : F=(B-A) / C
    : D=10^INT LOG F
 50 IF B < =D*INT (A / D)+CD THEN 80
 60 E=E+1
    : IF E / 4 < > INT (E / 4) LET D=8D / 5
 70 D=5D/4
    : GOTO 50
 80 A=D*INT (A / D)
    : B=A+CD
    : C=(B-A) / C
 90 PRINT"START AT ";A
100 PRINT"END AT ";B
110 PRINT"INCREMENT= ";C
    : GOTO 1
```

Graphing Helper—Plotting a Function

This program provides help with plotting a function. Two modes are available. You may input X values one at a time for analysis, or a range of X values, with a chosen increment, may be analyzed. Example: Plot the function $Y = 3X^2 - 2X + 7$

Display		You Enter
>>>		FUN
X?		−2
−2.	23.	ENTER
X?		0
0.	7.	ENTER
X?		ENTER
A?		0
B?		2
INC?		.2
0.	7.	ENTER
0.2	6.72	ENTER
0.4	6.68	ENTER
0.6	6.88	ENTER
0.8	7.32	ENTER
1.	8.	ENTER
1.2	8.92	ENTER
1.4	10.08	ENTER
1.6	11.48	ENTER
1.8	13.12	ENTER
2.	15.	ENTER
X?		ENTER
A?		ENTER
>>>		

Program length is 118 steps.

LISTING

```
10 "FUN"INPUT"X?",X
   : GOSUB"FX"
   : PRINT X,Y
   : GOTO 10
20 INPUT"A?",A,"B?",B,"INC?",C
   : FOR D=0 TO (B−A) / C
```

```
    : X=A+CD
    : GOSUB"FX"
    . PRINT X,Y
    : NEXT D
    : GOTO 10
 30 GOTO 1
900 "FX"Y=3XX-2X+7
    : RETURN
```

Greatest Common Divisor

This program computes the greatest common divisor of two integers. For example: Compute the GCD of 51 and 119.

Display	You Enter
>>>	GCD
?	51
?	119
GCD= 17.	ENTER
>>>	

Program length is 57 steps.

LISTING

```
10 "GCD"INPUT X,Y
20 Z=X-Y*INT (X / Y)
   : X=Y
   : Y=Z
   : IF Z THEN 20
30 PRINT"GCD= ";X
   : GOTO 1
```

Gudermannian Function and Inverse

This pair of programs computes the Gudermannian function and its inverse. (Fig. 15) The computer may be set in any angular mode. Example: Compute gd(2) and $gd^{-1}(1)$. RAD mode is set.

Display	You Enter
>>>	GD
?	2
1.301760336	ENTER
>>>	IGD
?	1
1.226191171	ENTER
>>>	

Program length is 49 steps.

LISTING

```
10 "GD"INPUT X
   : PRINT 2*ATN EXP X-2*ATN 1
   : GOTO 1
20 "IGD"INPUT X
   : PRINT LN TAN(ATN 1+X / 2)
   : GOTO 1
```

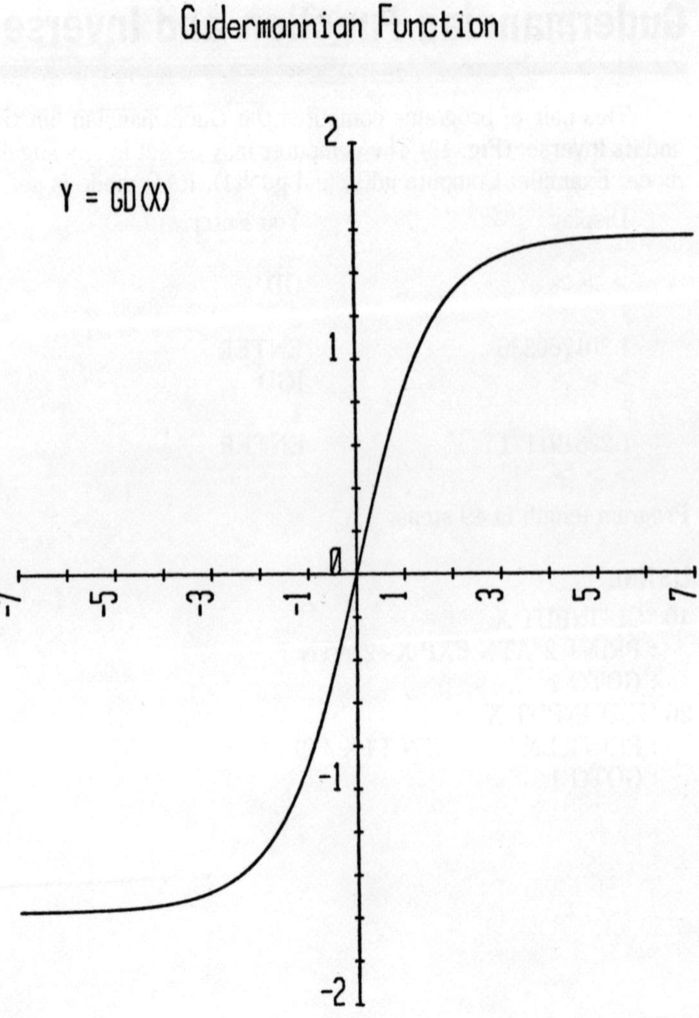

Fig. 15.

Histogram Bins

This program tallies numbers into bins for producing a histogram. The bin width and range values are input, followed by the list of numbers to be tallied. Bin boundaries and the tally are output for each bin. For instance: Draw a histogram of the twenty four student scores that follow. Use a bin width of 10. (Fig. 16)

Scores —
54, 77, 23, 19, 71, 34, 46, 42, 7, 96, 31, 59,
69, 67, 84, 12, 39, 55, 65, 55, 65, 84, 53, 42

Display	You Enter
> > >	HB
BIN WIDTH?	10
STARTING AT?	0
VALUE?	54
VALUE?	77
VALUE?	23
(etc.)	
VALUE?	53
VALUE?	42
VALUE?	ENTER
BIN RANGE– >	ENTER
0. 10.	ENTER
TALLY= 1.	ENTER
BIN RANGE– >	ENTER
10. 20.	ENTER
TALLY= 2.	ENTER

(etc.)

Program length is 183 steps.

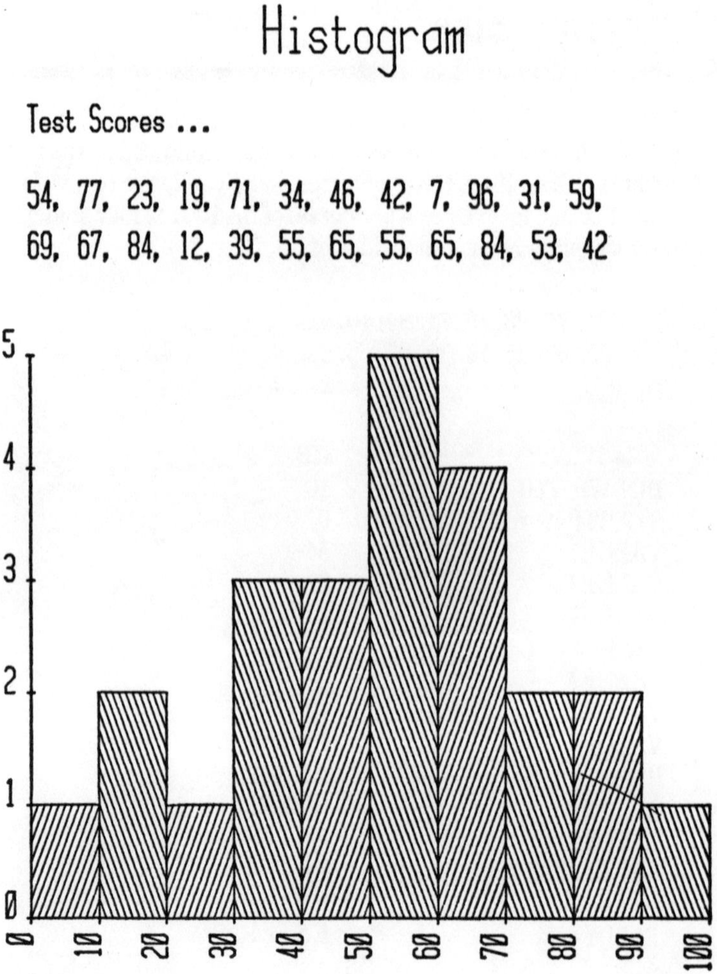
Histogram
Test Scores ...
54, 77, 23, 19, 71, 34, 46, 42, 7, 96, 31, 59,
69, 67, 84, 12, 39, 55, 65, 55, 65, 84, 53, 42
5
4
3
2
1
0
0
10
20
30
40
50
60
70
80
90
100

Fig. 16.

LISTING

```
10 "HB"CLEAR
   : G=7
   : INPUT"BIN WIDTH?",B,"STARTING AT?",C
20 INPUT"VALUE?",D
   : E=INT ( (D-C) / B)+8
   : A(E)=A(E)+1
   : F=F*(E < =F) + E*(E > F)
   GOTO 20
30 G=G+1
   : IF G > F THEN 1
40 D=BG-8B+C
   : E=D+B
   : PRINT"BIN RANGE- >"
50 PRINT D,E
   : PRINT"TALLY= ";A(G)
   : GOTO 30
```

Hyperbolic Functions

This collection of programs computes six of the hyperbolic functions.

$$SINH\,(X) = \frac{e^x - e^{-x}}{2} \qquad ASNH(X) = LN(X + \sqrt{}(X^2 + 1))$$

$$COSH\,(X) = \frac{e^x + e^{-x}}{2} \qquad ACSH(X) = LN\,(X + \sqrt{}(X^2 - 1))$$

$$TANH(X) = \frac{SINH\,(X)}{COSH(X)} \qquad ATNH(X) = \frac{LN\left(\frac{1 + X}{1 - X}\right)}{2}$$

For instance: Compute SINH(3).

Display	You Enter
> > >	SINH
?	3
10.01787493	ENTER
> > >	

Program length is 173 steps.

LISTING

```
10 "SINH"INPUT X
   : PRINT (EXP X–EXP–X) / 2
   : GOTO 1
20 "COSH"INPUT X
   : PRINT (EXP X+EXP–X) / 2
   : GOTO 1
30 "TANH"INPUT X
   : PRINT (EXP X–EXP–X) / (EXP X+EXP–X)
   : GOTO 1
40 "ASNH"INPUT X
   : PRINT LN(X+ √(XX+1))
   : GOTO 1
50 "ACSH"INPUT X
   : PRINT LN(X+ √(XX–1))
   : GOTO 1
```

```
60 "ATNH"INPUT X
   : PRINT LN((1+X) / (1-X)) / 2
   : GOTO 1
```

Integrals—Cosine Integral

This program computes the cosine integral of X. (Fig. 17)

$$Ci(X) = \int_{\infty}^{x} \frac{\cos t}{t}\, dt$$

Example: Compute Ci(.2)

Display	You Enter
> > >	CI
?	.2
−1.042205596	ENTER
> > >	

Program length is 115 steps.

LISTING

```
10 "CI"INPUT X
   : F=1
   : N=0
   : C=0
20 Y=C
   : N=N+1
   : M=2N
   : F=FM*(M-1)
30 P=N / 2
   : P=INT P=P
   : P=2P-1
   : C=C+PX^M / M / F
   : IF C < > Y THEN 20
40 PRINT C+LN X+.5772156649
   : GOTO 1
```

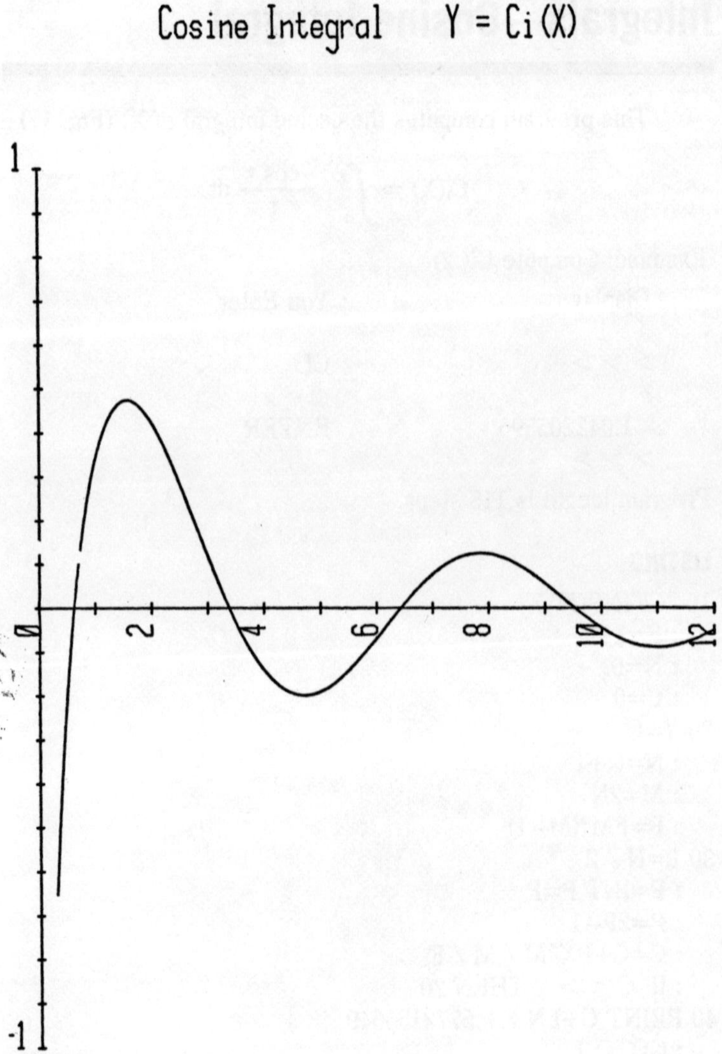

Fig. 17

Integrals—Exponential Integral

This program computes the exponential integral of X. (Fig. 18)

$$Ei(X) = \int_{-\infty}^{x} \frac{EXP(t)}{t} dt$$

Example: Compute Ei(1.7)

Display	You Enter
>>>	EI
?	1.7
3.9209632	ENTER
>>>	

Program length is 81 steps.

LISTING

```
10 "EI"INPUT X
   : F=1
   : E=0
   : N=0
20 Y=E
   : N=N+1
   : F=FN
   : E=E+X^N / N / F
   : IF E < > Y THEN 20
30 PRINT E+LN X+ .5772156649
   : GOTO 1
```

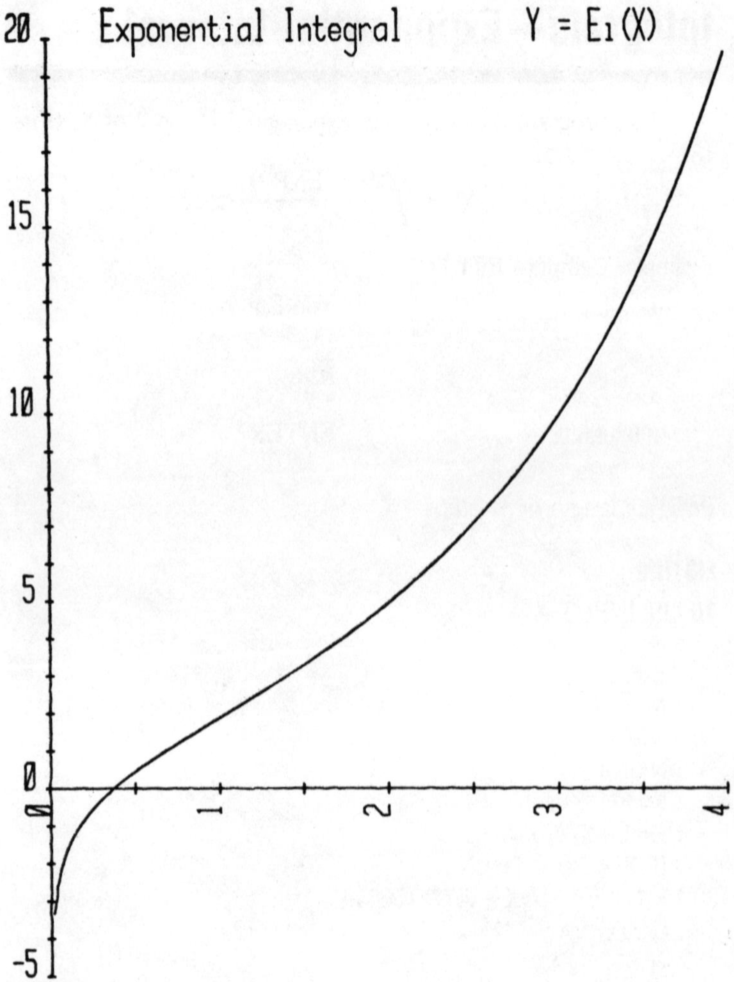

Fig. 18.

Integrals—Sine Integral

This program computes the sine integral of X. (Fig. 19)

$$Si(X) = \int_{\phi}^{x} \frac{SIN\ (t)}{t}\ dt$$

Example: Compute Si(6.9)

Display	You Enter
> > >	SI
?	6.9
1.445702443	ENTER
> > >	

Program length is 107 steps.

LISTING

```
10 "SI"INPUT X
   : F=1
   : N=0
   : S=0
20 Y=S
   : M=2N+1
   : IF M > 1 LET F=FM*(M-1)
30 P=N / 2
   : P=INT P=P
   : P=2P-1
   : S=S+PX^M / M / F
   : N=N+1
   : IF S < > Y  THEN 20
40 PRINT Y
   GOTO 1
```

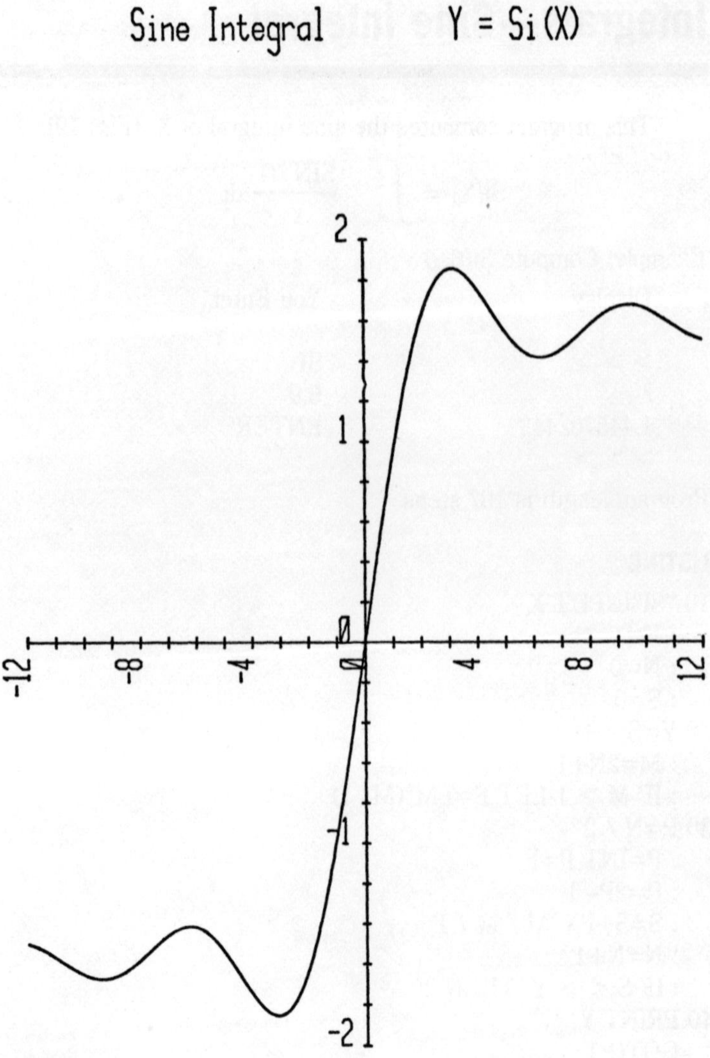

Fig. 19.

Integration—Gaussian Quadrature

This program computes an approximation for the definite integral of a function. Either a finite interval A to B, or an infinite interval from A to ∞ may be used.
First example: Integrate $Y=X^2$ from 1.1 to 1.7. (Fig. 20)

Display	You Enter
>>>	GQ
A?	1.1
B? (IF FINITE)	1.7
INTEGRL= 1.194	ENTER
>>>	

Second example: Integrate Y = EXP(−X) from 1 to infinity. (Fig. 21). First erase line 900, leaving line 910 as our function FX.

Display	You Enter
>>>	GQ
A?	1
B? (IF FINITE)	ENTER
INTEGRL= .3662854242	ENTER
>>>	

Program length is 333 steps.

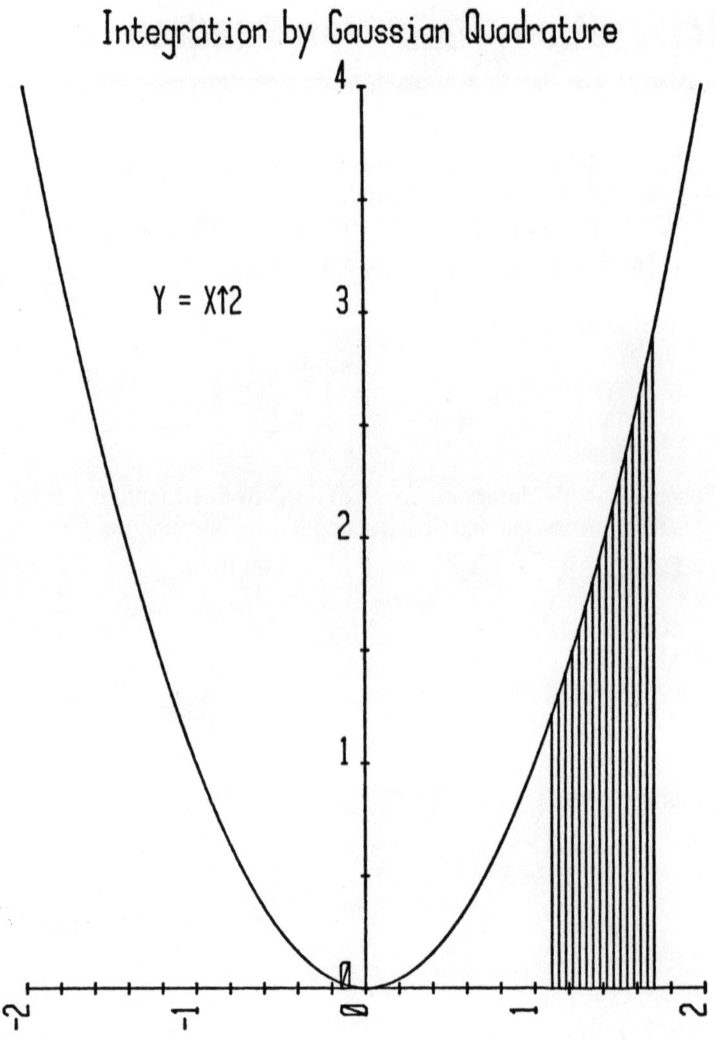

Fig. 20.

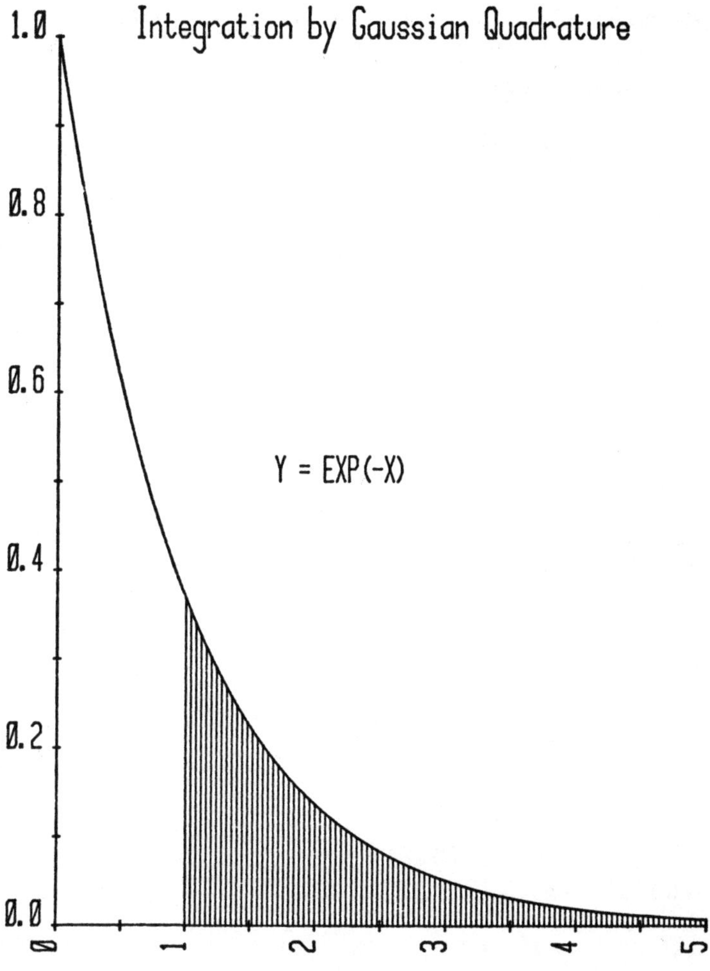

Integration by Gaussian Quadrature
1.0
0.8
0.6
0.4
0.2
0.0
Y = EXP(-X)
0
1
2
3
4
5

Fig. 21.

LISTING

```
10 "GQ"CLEAR
   : L=.4679139346
   : M=L
   : N=.360761573
   : O=N
20 P=.1713244924
   : Q=P
   : R= .2386191861
   : S=-R
30 T=.6612093865
   : U=-T
   : V=.9324695142
   : W=-V
40 INPUT"A?",A,"B? (IF FINITE)",B
   : C=1
50 FOR Z=12 TO 17
   : IF C LET X=(A(Z+6)*(B-A)+B+A) / 2
   : GOTO 70
60 X=2 / (1+A(Z+6))+A-1
70 GOSUB"FX"
   : J=YA(Z)
   : IF C=0 LET J=J / (1+A(Z+6))^2
80 K=K+J
   : NEXT Z
   : K=2K
   : IF C LET K=K*(B-A) / 4
90 PRINT"INTEGRL= ";K
   : GOTO 1
900 "FX"Y=XX
   : RETURN
910 "FX"Y=EXP-X
   : RETURN
```

Integration—Simpson's Rule

This program approximates the integral of a function from A to B by Simpson's rule.

$$\int_A^B F(X) \cong \frac{H}{3}\left[F(A)+4F(A+H)+2F(A+2H)+4F(A+3H)+\ldots+2F(B-2H)+4F(B-H)+F(B)\right]$$

$$\text{where } H = \frac{B-A}{N}$$

Example: Integrate $Y = 3X^2 - 2X + 7$ from -1.5 to $-.7$ using 20 intervals. (Fig. 22)

Display	You Enter
>>>	SIMP
A?	−1.5
B?	−.7
N?	20
INTEGRL= 10.392	ENTER
>>>	

Program length is 163 steps.

LISTING

```
 10 "SIMP"INPUT"A?",A,"B?",B,"N?",N
    : N=2*INT(N / 2)
    : H=(B-A) / N
    : F=1
    : K=0
 20 FOR Z=0 TO N
    : F=0=F
    : X=A+ZH
    : GOSUB "FX"
    : K=K+2Y+2YF-Y*((Z=0)+(Z=N))
    : NEXT Z
 30 K=KH / 3
    : PRINT"INTEGRL= ";K
    : GOTO 1
900 "FX"Y=3XX-2X+7
    : RETURN
```

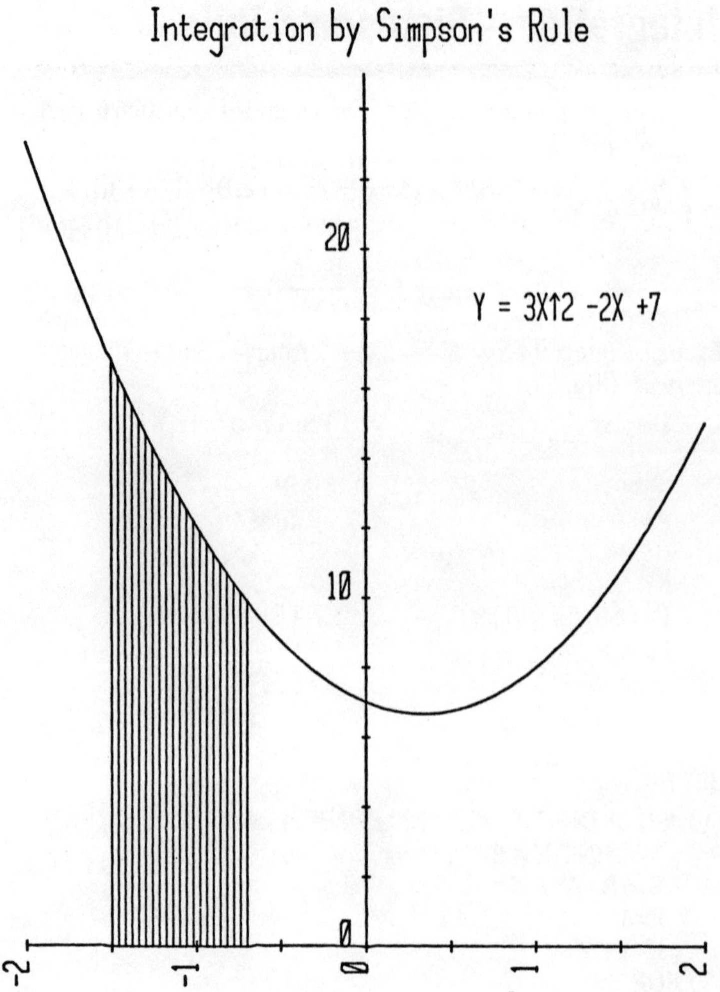

Fig. 22.

Integration—Weddle's Rule

This program finds the approximate area under a curve by "Weddle's Rule". This method is faster and more accurate than either Simpson's Rule or the Trapezoidal Rule for many functions. The example solution is accurate to the full eight decimal places shown.

$$\int_A^B F(X) \simeq \frac{3H}{10}\left[\begin{array}{l}F(A)+5F(A+H)+6F(A+3H)+F(A\\+4H)+5F(A+5H)+F(B)\end{array}\right]$$

$$\text{where } H = \frac{B-A}{6}$$

Example: Find where $f(x) = 1.26X^5 - 3.7X^4 - 8X^3 + 14X^2 + 10X + 4$. (Refer to Fig. 23)

Display	You Enter
>>>	WEDD
A?	−1
B?	.7
(Approximately twenty second delay)	
INTEGRAL= 10.94335027	ENTER
>>>	

The function to be integrated should be labeled "FX" and should return a single value in variable Y. Refer to line 900 of the example. Modify this line for your own functions.

Take a close look at the third segment of line 20.

```
:F=0=F
```

The value of F is toggled between 0 and 1 each time this statement is executed. Translated to a more standard BASIC it says:

```
IF F=0 LET F=1 ELSE LET F=0
```

A similar technique is used in the next segment of line 20.

```
K=K+Y+4FY+Y*(Z=3)
```

Recalling that the result of a "true or false" test is always either 1 or 0, this translates to:

```
LET K=K+Y+4FY
IF Z=3 LET K=K+Y
```

This same technique of using logical expressions is used in several other programs in this book.

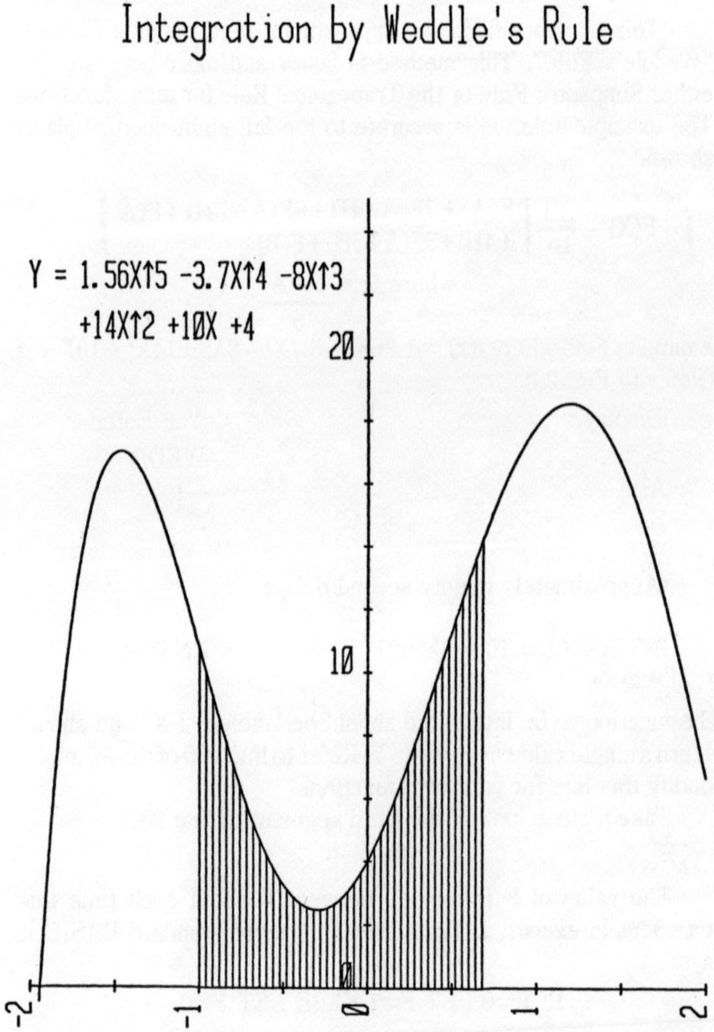

Fig. 23.

LISTING

```
 10 "WEDD"INPUT"A?",A,"B?",B
    : H=(B–A) / 6
    : F=1
    : K=0
    : FOR Z=0 TO 6
 20 X=A+ZH
    : GOSUB"FX"
    : F=0=F
    : K=K+Y+4FY+Y*(Z=3)
    : NEXT Z
 30 K=3HK / 10
    : PRINT"INTEGRL= ";K
    : GOTO 1
900 "FX"Y=1.56XXXXX–3.7XXXX–8XXX+14XX+10X+4
    : RETURN
```

Interpolation—Lagrange

This program uses Lagrange interpolation to compute an approximation of Y for a given X. All of the known X,Y points are used for the interpolation.

Example: Interpolate Y at X = 2.3 given the three points (−1,1), (1,1) and (3,9).

Display	You Enter
>>>	LGI
KNOWN X?	−1
AND Y?	1
KNOWN X?	1
AND Y?	1
KNOWN X?	3
AND Y?	9
KNOWN X?	ENTER
NEW X?	2.3
2.3 5.29	ENTER
NEW X?	ENTER
>>>	

Program length is 187 steps.

LISTING

```
10 "LGI"CLEAR
20 B=2A+9
   : C=B+1
   : INPUT"KNOWN X?",A(B),"AND Y?",A(C)
   : A=A+1
   : GOTO 20
30 H=0
   : INPUT"NEW X?",B
   : GOTO 50
40 GOTO 1
50 FOR C=1 TO A
   : D=1
   : E=2C+7
   : FOR F=1 TO A
60 G=2F+7
   : IF C < > F LET D=(DB−DA(G)) / (A(E)−A(G))
```

```
70 NEXT F
   : H=H+DA(E+1)
   : NEXT C
   : PRINT B,H
   : GOTO 30
```

Interpolation—Linear

This program computes a third point along a line determined by two given points. The third point may be determined by inputting either X or Y. For instance: Determine Y at X=2.3 if the first given point is −1, 1 and the second point is 3,9. (Fig. 24)

Display	You Enter
>>>	LI
X1?	−1
Y1?	1
X2?	3
Y2?	9
X?	2.3
2.3 6.6	ENTER
>>>	

Or, the X,Y values of the third point are 2.3, 6.6
Program length is 113 steps.

LISTING

```
10 "LI"INPUT"X1?",A,"Y1?",B,"X2?",C,"Y2?",D
20 INPUT"X?", X
   : Y=(D-B)*(X-A) / (C-A)
   : GOTO 40
30 INPUT"Y?",Y
   : X=(C-A)*(Y-B) / (D-B)
40 PRINT X,Y
   : GOTO 1
```

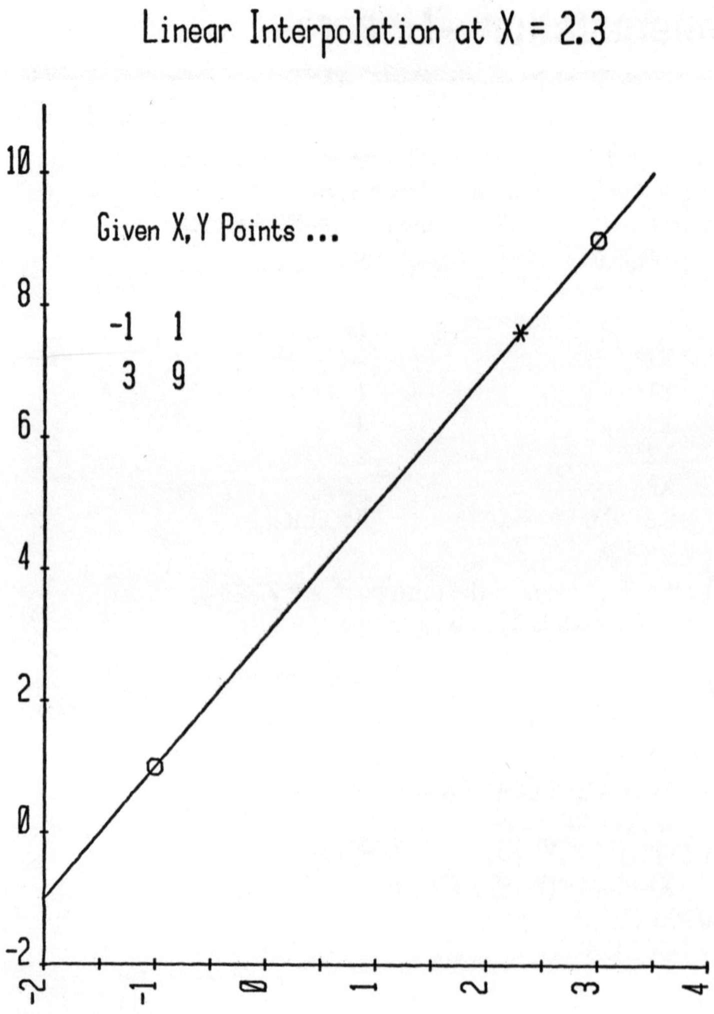

Linear Interpolation at X = 2.3
Given X,Y Points ...
-1 1
3 9
10
8
6
4
2
0
-2
-2
-1
0
1
2
3
4

Fig. 24.

Least Common Multiple

This program computes the least common multiple of two integers. For example: Compute the LCM of 51 and 119.

Display	You Enter
>>>	LCM
?	51
?	119
LCM= 357.	ENTER
>>>	

Program length is 75 steps.

LISTING

```
10 "LCM"INPUT X,Y
   : A=X
   : B=Y
20 Z=X-Y*INT(X / Y)
   : X=Y
   : Y=Z
   : IF Z THEN 20
30 Z=ABS(AB / X)
   : PRINT"LCM= ";Z
   : GOTO 1
```

Least Common Multiple

Limit of a Function

This program demonstrates the limit of a function near a point. With each iteration the function is evaluated closer to the given point, both from the left and from the right. Example: What is the limit of SIN(X) / X as X approaches zero? (Notice that at X=0 the function is undefined.)

Display	You Enter
>>>	LIM
LIMIT AT X=?	0
FROM LEFT, FROM RIGHT	
6.36619 E−01 6.36619 E−01	ENTER
FROM LEFT, FROM RIGHT	
9.00316 E−01 9.00316 E−01	ENTER
FROM LEFT, FROM RIGHT	
9.74495 E−01 9.74495 E−01	ENTER
FROM LEFT, FROM RIGHT	
9.93586 E−01 9.93586 E−01	ENTER
(etc.)	

The limit appears to be approaching 1.
Program length is 151 steps.

LISTING

```
 10 "LIM"INPUT"LIMIT AT X=?",Z
    : L=Z- π
    : R=Z+ π
 20 L=(L+Z) / 2
    : R=(R+Z) / 2
 30 X=L
    : GOSUB"FX"
    : A=Y
 40 X=R
    : GOSUB"FX"
    : B=Y
 50 PAUSE"FROM LEFT, FROM RIGHT"
    : PRINT A,B
    : GOTO 20
900 "FX"RADIAN
    : Y=SIN X / X
    : RETURN
```

Line Analysis

This program simplifies the analysis of straight lines in the X,Y plane. An X,Y point is entered and then any two of the following three variables. The slope, an X coordinate, and a Y coordinate. For instance; A line passes through the points (−4, 1.4) and (2, −2.2). Compute the slope and Y intercept for this line.

Display	You Enter
>>>	LN
X1?	−4
Y1?	1.4
SLOPE?	ENTER
X2?	2
Y2?	−2.2
−4. 1.4	ENTER
2 −2.2	ENTER
SLOPE= −0.6	ENTER
>>>	LN
X1?	−4
Y1?	1.4
SLOPE?	−.6
X2?	0
−4. 1.4	ENTER
0 −1.	ENTER (at X=0 then Y=−1)
SLOPE= −0.6	ENTER
>>>	

Program length is 152 steps.

LISTING

```
10 "LN"CLEAR
  : INPUT"X1?",X,"Y1?",Y
20 INPUT"SLOPE?",M,"X2?",A
  : B=MA−MX+Y
  : GOTO 50
30 IF M INPUT"Y2?",B
  : A=(MX+B−Y) / M
  : GOTO 50
40 INPUT"X2?",A,"Y2?",B
  : M=(Y−B) / (X−A)
```

```
50 PRINT X,Y
   : PRINT A,B
   : PRINT"SLOPE= ";M
   : GOTO 1
```

Loan

This program flexibly solves most questions related to borrowing money. You input any four of the following five variables and the fifth will be computed. They are:

1. Principal
2. Yearly interest rate
3. Number of years for the loan
4. Number of payments per year
5. Amount of each payment

Just press ENTER when prompted for the unknown. Example: What would the monthly payments be for a three year loan of $2000 at 13.5% interest?

Display	You Enter
> > >	LOAN
PRINCIPAL?	2000
YEARLY INTEREST RATE?	13.5
# YEARS FOR LOAN?	3
# PAYMENTS / YEAR?	12
PAYMENT AMOUNT?	ENTER
PRINCIPAL= 2000.	ENTER
YEARLY INTEREST= 13.5	ENTER
YEARS FOR LOAN= 3.	ENTER
#PAYMENTS / YEAR= 12.	ENTER
PAYMENT AMT= 67.87	ENTER

Program length is 528 steps.

LISTING

```
10 "LOAN"CLEAR
   : Z=100
   : INPUT"PRINCIPAL?",P
20 INPUT"YEARLY INTEREST RATE?",I
30 INPUT"# YEARS FOR LOAN?",Y
40 INPUT"# PAYMENTS / YEAR?",N
50 INPUT"PAYMENT AMOUNT?",A
60 I=I / Z
   : IF A=0 LET M=1-(I / N+1)^-NY
   : A=IP / M / N
   : GOTO 150
```

```
70 IF Y=0 LET Y=-LN(1-PI / N / A) / N / LN(1+I / N)
   : GOTO 150
80 IF P=0 LET P=AN*(1-(I / N+1) -NY) / I
   : GOTO 150
90 IF N THEN 120
100 N=N+(N=0)
   : N=IP / A / (1-(I / N+1)^-NY)
   : IF INT ZN=INT M THEN 150
110 M=ZN
   : GOTO 100
120 K=K+Z*(K=0)
   : I=(J+K) / 2
   : M=1-(I / N+1)^-NY
   : L=IP / M / N-A
   : IF K-J < 1 / Z THEN 150
130 IF L LET K=I
   : GOTO 120
140 J=I
   : GOTO 120
150 PRINT"PRINCIPAL= ";P
   : I=ZI
   : PRINT"YEARLY INTEREST= ";I
160 PRINT"YEARS FOR LOAN= ";Y
   : PRINT"# PAYMENTS / YEAR= ";N
170 A=INT AZ / Z
   : PRINT"PAYMENT AMT= ";A
   : GOTO 1
```

Logarithms to Any Base

Your TRS-80 Pocket Computer has two built in logarithm functions, LOG for base 10, and LN for base 2.718281828 (called the natural log and represented by *e*). Using the following formula it's easy to compute the logarithm function for any base.

$$LOG_b(X) = LOG_e(X) / LOG_e(b)$$

For instance: Compute LOG_2 (256).

Display	You Enter
>>>	LB
X?	256
BASE?	2
8.	ENTER
>>>	

Or, LOG_2 (256) = 8.

Program length is 34 steps.

LISTING

```
10 "LB"INPUT"X?",X,"BASE?",B
: PRINT LN X / LN B
: GOTO 1
```

Matrix Inversion

This program computes the inverse of a square matrix. The size of the matrix is limited only by available memory. During data entry you can verify where you're at by just pressing ENTER. The position of the next value to be entered will be displayed. When the inversion is complete you'll hear a beep. The position in the matrix and the value is displayed sequentially for each value. "2.3.)= 3.14" indicates that the value in the second row and third column of the inverted matrix is 3.14. To review the solution, rerun the output, starting at MATOUT. Example: Invert the following matrix.

1	2
3	4

Display	You Enter
> > >	MATI
SIZE?	2
?	1
?	2
?	ENTER
DOWN2. ACROSS1.	
?	3
?	4
BEEP	
1.1.) = −2.	ENTER
1.2.)= 1.	ENTER
2.1.)= 1.5	ENTER
2.2.)=−0.5	ENTER
> > >	

Program length is 528 steps.

LISTING

```
10 "MATI"CLEAR
   : INPUT"SIZE?",A
   : A(2AA+8)=0
   : B=AA+8
   : FOR E=1 TO A
   : FOR F=1 TO A
   : B=B+1
   : A(B)=(E=F)
```

```
20 INPUT A(EA+F−A+8)
   : NEXT F
   : NEXT E
   : GOTO 40
30 PAUSE"DOWN ";E;" ACROSS ";F
   : GOTO 20
40 FOR F=1 TO A
   : E=F
50 IF ABS A(EA+F−A+8) GOTO 80
60 E=E+1
   : IF E <=A THEN 50
70 PRINT"SINGULAR"
   : GOTO 1
80 FOR G=1 TO A
   : B=FA+G−A+8
   : C=EA+G−A+8
   : D=A(B)
   : A(B)=A(C)
   : A(C)=D
90 B=B+AA
   : C=C+AA
   : D=A(B)
   : A(B)=A(C)
   : A(C)=D
   : NEXT G
100 B=A(FA+F−A+8)
   : FOR G=1 TO A
   : C=FA+G−A+8
   : D=C+AA
   : A(C)=A(C) / B
110 A(D)=A(D) / B
   : NEXT G
   : FOR H=1 TO A
   : IF H=F THEN 140
120 B=A(HA+F−A+8)
   : FOR G=1 TO A
   : C=HA+G−A+8
   : D=FA+G−A+8
130 A(C)=A(C)−BA(D)
   : C=C+AA
   : A(C)=A(C)−BA(D+AA)
   : NEXT G
```

```
140 NEXT H
    : NEXT F
    : BEEP 1
150 "MATOUT"FOR E=1 TO A
    : FOR F=1 TO A
    : B=EA+F-A+8+AA
    : PRINT E;F;")= ";A(B)
    : NEXT F
    : NEXT E
    : GOTO 1
```

Mean And Standard Deviation— Grouped Data

This program computes the mean and standard deviation for grouped data.
Given a set of data $(X_1, X_2, X_3, \ldots X_n)$
with frequencies $(F_1, F_2, F_3, \ldots F_n)$

$$\text{Mean} = \sum_{i=1}^{n} F_i X_i \Big/ \sum_{i=1}^{n} F_i$$

$$\text{Standard Deviation} = \sqrt{\left[\frac{\sum_{i=1}^{n} F_i X_i^2 - \left(\sum_{i=1}^{n} F_i X_i\right)^2 / K}{K}\right]}$$

$$\text{where } K = \sum_{i=1}^{n} F_i$$

Example: Compute the mean and standard deviation for the following grouped data.

X_i	10	20	30
F_i	4	5	5

Display	You Enter
>>>	MSDG
X?	10
FREQ?	4
X?	20
FREQ?	5
X?	30
FREQ?	5
X?	ENTER
MEAN= 20.71428571	ENTER
S.D.=8.287419302	ENTER
>>>	

Program length is 112 steps.

LISTING

```
10 "MSDG"CLEAR
20 INPUT"X?",X,"FREQ?",F
   : A=A+F
   : B=B+FX
   : C=C+FXX
   : GOTO 20
30 M=B / A
   : S= √( (C–BB / A)  /  (A–1) )
40 PRINT"MEAN= ";M
   : PRINT"S.D.= ";S
   : GOTO 1
```

Mean and Standard Deviation—Ungrouped Data

This program computes the mean and standard deviation for ungrouped data. Given a set of data ($X_1, X_2, X_3, \ldots X_n$):

$$\text{Mean} = \frac{\sum_{i=1}^{n} X_i}{n}$$

$$\text{Standard Deviation} = \sqrt{\left[\frac{\sum_{i=1}^{n} \quad \left(\sum_{i=1}^{n} X_i\right)^2 / n}{n-1}\right]}$$

Example: Compute the mean and standard deviation for the following data.

X_i 10 20 30 35

Display	You Enter
>>>	MSD
X?	10
X?	20
X?	30
X?	35
X?	ENTER
MEAN= 23.75	ENTER
S.D.=11.08677891	ENTER
>>>	

Program length is 99 steps.

LISTING

```
10 "MSD"CLEAR
20 INPUT"X?",X
   : A=A+1
   : B=B+X
   : C=C+XX
   : GOTO 20
30 M=B / A
   : S= √( (C–BB / A) / (A–1))
40 PRINT"MEAN= ";M
   : PRINT"S.D.= ";S
   : GOTO 1
```

Means—Arithmetic, Geometric, And Harmonic

This program computes three types of means for a group of numbers. (X_1, X_2, X_3, . . . X_n):

$$\text{Arithmetic mean} = \frac{1}{n} \sum_{i=1}^{n} X_i$$

$$\text{Geometric mean} = \sqrt[n]{(X_1 * X_2 * X_3 * \ldots * X_n)}$$

$$\text{Harmonic mean} = n \Big/ \left(\sum_{i=1}^{n} \frac{1}{X_i} \right)$$

Example: What are the three means for 7, 9, 12, 15, and 17?

Display	You Enter
>>>	MNS
X?	7
X?	9
X?	12
X?	15
X?	17
X?	ENTER
ARTH MN= 12.	ENTER
GEOM MN= 11.40282332	ENTER
HRMNC MN= 10.80399475	ENTER
>>>	

Program length is 127 steps.

LISTING

```
10 "MNS"CLEAR
   : C=1
20 INPUT"X?",X
   : A=A+1
   : B=B+X
   : C=CX
   : D=D+1 / X
   : GOTO 20
```

```
30 B=B / A
   : C=C^(1 / A)
   : D=A / D
   : PRINT"ARTH MN= ";B
40 PRINT"GEOM MN= ";C
   : PRINT"HRMNC MN= ";D
   : GOTO 1
```

Metric Conversions

This program demonstrates a technique for programming metric conversions. Two sample conversions are given, gallons / liters and miles / kilometers. Follow the same format as in lines 10 and 20 to create your own conversions.

Two numbers are displayed after each conversion. This is because the conversion computes in both directions simultaneously. Follow the example to see this better. Notice that the title of each routine indicates the order of the conversions.

For example: How many liters in 7 gallons?

Display	You Enter
>>>	G.L
?	7
1.849204367 26.49788249	ENTER
>>>	

We want gallons converted to liters, so 26.49788249 is our answer. (The other answer tells us there are 1.849204367 gallons in 7 liters).

Program length is 67 steps. Each additional conversion requires approximately 20 to 25 steps.

LISTING

```
10 "G.L"K=3.785411784
   : GOTO 99
20 "M.K"K=1.609344
   : GOTO 99
99 INPUT X
   : Y=KX
   : PRINT X / K,Y
   : GOTO 1
```

Metric Conversions

[illegible]

For example: How many liters in 7 gallons?

[illegible]

LISTING

[illegible]

Miles Per Gallon

This program helps keep track of your vehicle's rate of fuel consumption. For each fill up you enter the gallons of gas and the odometer reading. The miles per gallon since the last fill up and the miles per gallon since you started keeping track are displayed.

Display	You Enter
> > >	MPG
ODOMETER? (FIRST FILL)	12345
GAL?	9.6
ODOMETER?	12527
MPG THIS TANK= 18.9	ENTER
MPG OVERALL= 18.9	ENTER
GAL?	7
ODOMETER?	12703
MPG THIS TANK= 25.1	ENTER
MPG OVERALL= 21.5	ENTER
GAL?	
(etc.)	

Program length is 158 steps.

LISTING

```
10 "MPG"INPUT"ODOMETER? (FIRST FILL)",M
   : A=M
   : T=0
20 INPUT"GAL?",G,"ODOMETER?",N
30 P=(N-M) / G
   : M=N
   : T=T+G
   : Q=(N-A) / T
   : USING"# # # . #"
40 PRINT"MPG THIS TANK= ";P
50 PRINT"MPG OVERALL= ";Q
   : GOTO 20
```

Miles Per Hour

This program will help you calibrate your speedometer in your vehicle. Usually it's best to use one or two miles for the check, but if you can "hold 'er steady" for four or five miles the accuracy increases. Press ENTER as you pass a mile marker. Keep your speed steady. As you pass the final mile marker the display will indicate your actual speed. Compare this with the speedometer reading.

The value of C in line 10 determines the accuracy of this program. Try a five mile check and see if "60 MPH IF THERE" occurs after exactly five minutes. Adjust C if necessary.

Display	You Enter
>>>	MPH
MILES FOR CHECK?	2
ENTER TO START	ENTER
2325.5 MPH IF THERE	
1550.3 MPH IF THERE	
1162.7 MPH IF THERE	
(etc.)	

Press ON to BREAK the program.
Program length is 108 steps.

LISTING

```
10 "MPH"INPUT"MILES FOR CHECK?",M
   : C=4.3E4 / M
   : T=C
   : USING"# # # # #.#"
   : INPUT"ENTER TO START",Z
20 T=T+C
   : PAUSE 1 / T; " MPH IF THERE"
   : GOTO 20
```

Moving Average

This program computes a moving average of the last N values entered. You choose N. Example: Compute the moving average for the following sequence of values. Use the last four values for each average.

127, 139, 128, 142, 153, 167

Display	You Enter
> > >	MAV
HOW MANY EACH AVERAGE?	4
VALUE?	127
THAT WAS ENTRY # 1.	ENTER
VALUE?	139
THAT WAS ENTRY # 2.	ENTER
VALUE?	128
THAT WAS ENTRY # 3.	ENTER
VALUE?	142
MOVING AVE= 134.	ENTER
VALUE?	153
MOVING AVE= 140.5	ENTER
VALUE?	167
MOVING AVE= 147.5	ON
BREAK AT 50	

Program length is 164 steps.

LISTING

```
10 "MAV"CLEAR
   : INPUT"HOW MANY EACH AVERAGE?",A
   : C=5
20 C=C+1
   : IF C > 5+A LET C=6
30 D=D-A(C)
   : INPUT"VALUE?",A(C)
   : D=D+A(C)
40 E=D / A
   : B=B+1
   : IF B < A PRINT"THAT WAS ENTRY # ";B
   : GOTO 20
50 PRINT"MOVING AVE= ";E
   : GOTO 20
```

Number Conversions— Binary to Decimal

This program converts positive binary integers to the decimal equivalent. For instance: Convert 11010_2 to decimal.

Display	You Enter
> > >	BD
BIN?	11010
(2)11010.=26.	ENTER
> > >	

Program length is 87 steps.

LISTING

```
10 "BD"INPUT"BIN?",A
   : B=1
   : D=0
   : C=A
20 E=A / 10
   : A=INT E
   : D=D+10B*(E-A)
   : B=2B
   : IF A THEN 20
30 PRINT" < 2 > ";C;"=";D
   : GOTO 1
```

Number Conversions— Decimal to Binary

This program converts positive decimal integers to the binary equivalent. For instance: Convert 123 to binary.

Display	You Enter
> > >	DB
DEC?	123
123. = < 2 > 1111011.	ENTER
> > >	

Program length is 82 steps.

LISTING

```
10 "DB"INPUT "DEC?",D
   : B=0
   : A=D
   : C=1
20 E=D / 2
   : D=INT E
   : B=B+C*(D < E)
   : C=10C
   : IF D THEN 20
30 PRINT A;"= < 2 > ";B
   : GOTO 1
```

Number Conversions—Decimal to Hexadecimal

This program converts positive decimal integers to hexadecimal numbers. The hexadecimal answers have their digits expressed in pairs. Hence, the digits "A" through "F" are represented as "10" through "15". Don't overlook this digit pairing in the answers. For example: Convert 18 and 123 to hexadecimal.

Display	You Enter
>>>	DH
DEC?	18
18.= < 16 > 102.	ENTER (Grouped in pairs this is 12_{16})
>>>	DH
DEC?	123
123.= < 16 > 711.	ENTER (Or, $7B_{16}$)
>>>	

Program length is 88 steps.

LISTING

```
10 "DH"INPUT"DEC?",D
   : B=0
   : A=D
   : C=1
20 E=D / 16
   : D=INT E
   : F=E-D
   : B=B+16FC
   : C=100C
   : IF D THEN 20
30 PRINT A;"= < 16 > ";B
   : GOTO 1
```

Number Conversions— Decimal To Octal

This program converts positive decimal integers to the octal equivalent. For instance: Convert 12345 to octal.

Display	You Enter
> > >	DO
DEC?	12345
12345.= < 8 > 30071.	ENTER
> > >	

Program length is 84 steps.

LISTING

```
10 "DO"INPUT"DEC?",D
   : B=0
   : A=D
   : C=1
20 E=D / 8
   : D=INT E
   : F=E-D
   : B=B+8FC
   : C=10C
   : IF D THEN 20
30 PRINT A; "= < 8 > ";B
   : GOTO 1
```

Number Conversions—Hexadecimal to Decimal

This program converts positive hexadecimal integers to their decimal equivalent. Enter the hexadecimal digits as paired characters. For instance, enter A_{16} as 10, and $17F_{16}$ as 010715.

Example: Convert $12BC_{16}$ to decimal.

Display	You Enter
> > >	HD
HEX?	01021112
< 16 > 1021112.=4796.	ENTER
> > >	

Program length is 93 steps.

LISTING

```
10 "HD"INPUT"HEX?",A
   : B=1
   : D=0
   : C=A
   : F=100
20 E=A / F
   : A=INT E
   : D=D+FB*(E–A)
   : B=16B
   : IF A THEN 20
30 PRINT" < 16 > ";C;"=";D
   : GOTO 1
```

Number Conversions—Octal to Decimal

This program converts positive octal integers to the decimal equivalent. For instance: Convert 30071_8 to decimal.

Display	You Enter
> > >	OD
OCT?	30071
< 8 > 30071. = 12345.	ENTER
> > >	

Program length is 87 steps.

LISTING

```
10 "OD"INPUT"OCT?",A
   : B=1
   : D=0
   : C=A
20 E=A / 10
   : A=INT E
   : D=D+10B*(E−A)
   : B=8B
   : IF A THEN 20
30 PRINT " < 8 > ";C;"=";D
   : GOTO 1
```

Permutations

This program computes the permutation function of two integers.

$${}_{A}P_{B} = \frac{A!}{(A-B)!}$$

For example: Compute ${}_{12}P_{7}$.

Display	You Enter
>>>	PERM
?	12
?	7
PERM= 3991680.	ENTER
>>>	

Program length is 51 steps.

LISTING

```
10 "PERM"INPUT Y,X
   : P=1
   : FOR Z=Y-X+1 TO Y
   : P=PZ
   : NEXT Z
   : PRINT"PERM= ";P
   : GOTO 1
```

PI—By Dartboard

This program is an example of the Monte Carlo method of computation. Random events, taken in large quantities, can provide useful data about complicated phenomenon. In this example we're investigating a rather simple phenomenon, the throwing of randomly aimed darts at a special dartboard.

Our dartboard is a square with an inscribed circle of radius 1. (Fig. 25) The square has an area of 4 units, the circle has an area of PI units. If enough randomly aimed darts are thrown, the ratio of the number of darts inside the circle to the total number of darts thrown will approach the ratio of the areas, or PI / 4. So you can multiply the in-the-circle / total-thrown ratio by 4 to get an approximation for PI.

To make our math simpler and faster for our program we modified the dartboard as in Figure 26. The square now has an area of 1, and the quarter circle has an area of PI / 4. The ratio of areas is identical to our original dartboard.

Display		You Enter
>>>		PI
DARTS=1	HITS=1	
π = 4.0000		
DARTS= 2	HITS= 1	
π = 2.0000		
. . . (After several iterations)		
DARTS= 50	HITS=37	
π = 2.9600		

Press ON to BREAK the action. A large number of throws is necessary for a good approximation. Program length is 153 steps.

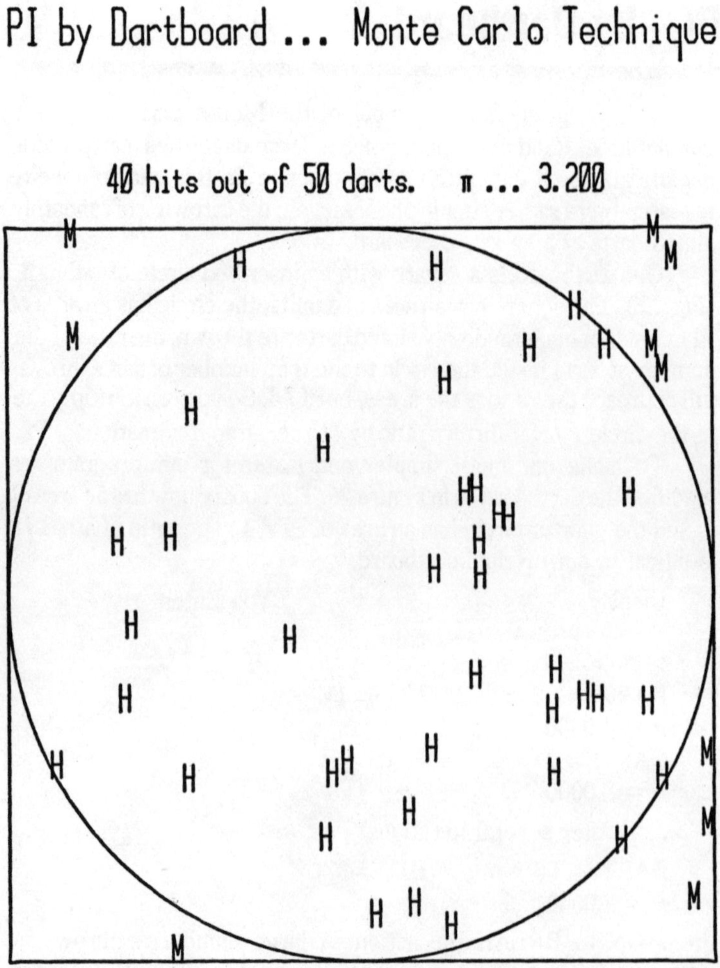
PI by Dartboard ... Monte Carlo Technique
40 hits out of 50 darts. π ... 3.200

Fig. 25.

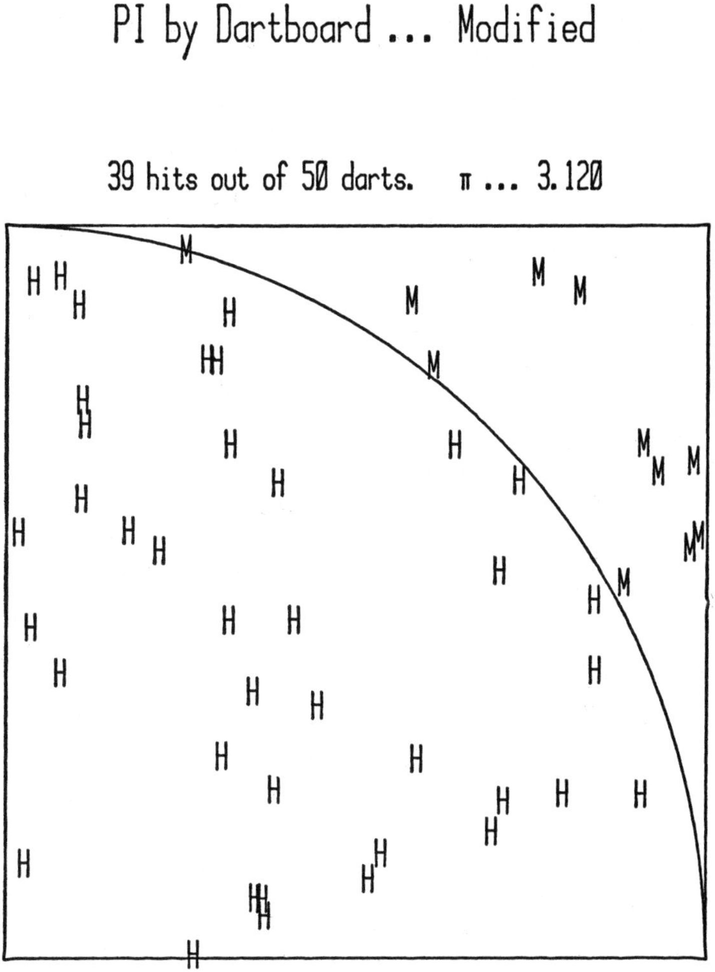

Fig. 26.

LISTING

```
 10 "PI"D=0
    : H=0
 20 GOSUB 100
    : S=R
    : GOSUB 100
 30 D=D+1
    : H=H+(SS+RR < 1)
 40 P=4H / D
 50 USING" # # # #"
 60 PAUSE"DARTS=";D;" HITS=";H
 70 USING"# #.# # # #"
 80 PAUSE" π = ";P
 90 GOTO 20
100 R = π + 983R
    : R=2*(R-INT R)-1
    : RETURN
```

Plotting—Three Dimensions

This program projects three dimensional points (X, Y, Z) onto the X, Y plane given the rotation and tilt angles you desire. By plotting these X, Y points, a view of three dimensional functions or objects can be created. Figure 27 is an example of the use of this algorithm on a larger and much faster computer. Your TRS-80 pocket computer is incapable of producing graphics of this nature, but by using this program for points in space at the ends of straight line segments, you can plot some very interesting views of three dimensional objects.

Example: Draw a cube rotated 27 degrees and tilted 17 degrees. (Fig. 28)

Display	You Enter
>>>	3D
ROTATION ANGLE?	27
TILT ANGLE?	17
X?	0
Y?	0
Z?	0
0. 0.	ENTER
X?	0
Y?	0
Z?	1
0. .956304756	ENTER
X?	0
Y?	1
Z?	0
– .45399 – .260505	ENTER
X?	1
Y?	0
Z?	0
.891006 –.132733	ENTER
X?	0
Y?	1
Z?	1
– .45399 .695799	ENTER
X?	1
Y?	1

Z?	0
.437016 −.393239	ENTER
X?	1
Y?	0
Z?	1
.891006 .82357	ENTER
X?	1
Y?	1
Z?	1
.437016 .563065	ENTER
X?	ENTER
> > >	

Program length is 115 steps.

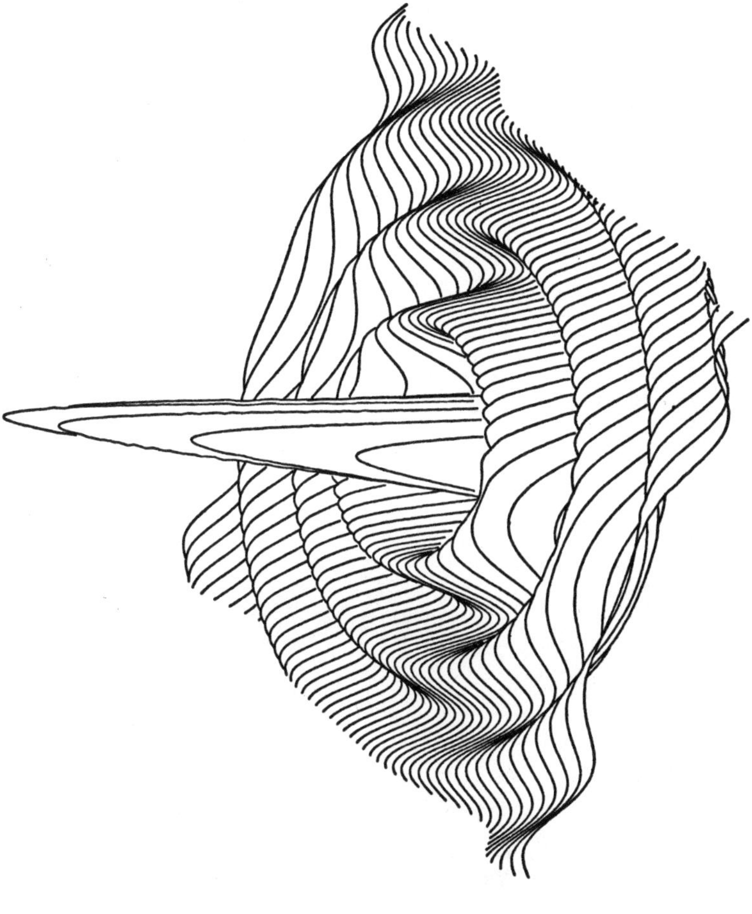

Fig. 27.

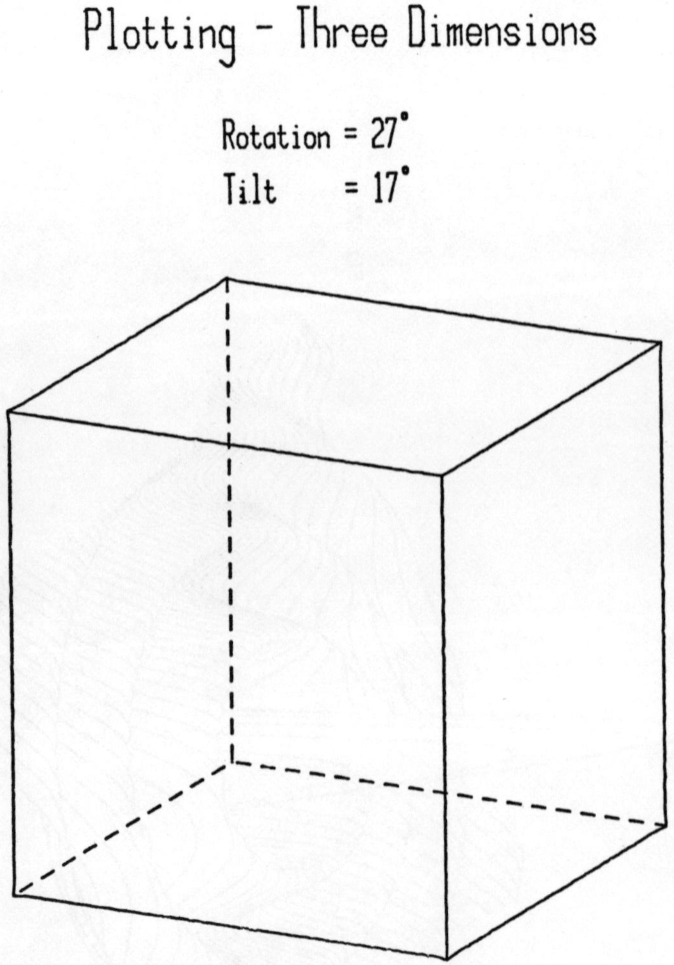

Fig. 28.

LISTING

```
10 "3D"INPUT"ROTATION ANGLE?",R,"TILT ANGLE?",T
20 INPUT"X?",X,"Y?",Y,"Z?",Z
   : A=X*COS R-Y*SIN R
   : B=Z*COS T-(X*SIN R+Y*COS R)*SIN T
   : PRINT A,B
   : GOTO 20
30 GOTO 1
```

Pocketext

This program is handy for grocery lists, telephone numbers, appointments, travel directions, advertising, etc. You might think of this program as the worlds smallest text editor.

There are actually three programs to work with. WRI creates all new text, REA displays the text, and EDI allows you to edit the text without having to erase everything.

WRI—Clears the flexible memory of your TRS-80. The fewer other programs you have loaded, the longer the text, you'll be able to store. With each "?" prompt enter up to 7 characters of text. Usually this is one word, but short words in pairs are okay. For instance, your first entries could be TRS 80, POCKET, and COMPUTR. After your last entry just press ENTER.

REA—Prints the text on the display. Groups of three strings from memory are displayed separated with spaces. For instance, if you had entered TRS 80, POCKET, and COMPUTR during the WRI program, then you would see TRS 80 POCKET COMPUTR as your first display. With each press of ENTER the next group of three strings is displayed.

EDI—Allows you to rewrite the text beginning at any chosen string. After locating the first occurrence of the string, the program branches into the WRI function. You may change one string this way, or you may write over all the remaining strings in the text.

For advertising purposes you might want the text to be displayed in a continuous loop mode. Two minor changes to the program and you're in business! Change the PRINT in line 70 to a PAUSE. and CHANGE line 80 to GOTO 50.

Display	You Enter
>>>	WRI
?	THIS
?	IS AN
?	EXAMPLE
?	FOR THE
?	TRS 80
?	POCKET
?	COMPUTR
?	POCKET –
?	TEXT
?	PROGRAM

```
?                                 ENTER
>>>                               REA
THIS IS AN EXAMPLE                ENTER
FOR THE TRS 80 POCKET             ENTER
COMPUTR POCKET - TEXT             ENTER
PROGRAM                           ENTER
>>>                               EDI
FIRST WORD TO REPLACE?            COMPUTR
?                                 CMPUTER
?                                 POCKET
?                                 ENTER
>>>                               REA
THIS IS AN EXAMPLE                ENTER
FOR THE TRS 80 POCKET             ENTER
CMPUTER POCKET-TEXT               ENTER
PROGRAM                           ENTER
>>>
```

Program length is 195 steps. Variable amount of flexible memory is required.

LISTING

```
 10 "WRI"CLEAR
    : A=26
 20 A=A+1
    : INPUT A$(A)
    : GOTO 20
 30 GOTO 1
 50 "REA"A=24
    :D$=" "
 60 A=A+3
    : B=A+1
    : C=A+2
 70 IF A$(A) PRINT A$(A);D$;A$(B);D$;A$(C)
    : GOTO 60
 80 GOTO 1
100 "EDI"A=27
    : INPUT"FIRST WORD TO REPLACE?",Z$
110 IF A$(A)=Z$ LET A=A-1
    : GOTO 20
120 A=A+1
    : GOTO 110
```

Pocket Alarm Clock

This program turns your TRS-80 pocket computer into a TRS-80 alarm clock! You'll be gently nudged into consciousness by twelve little beeps (one every five seconds for a minute).

Adjust the accuracy of the time keeping by tweeking the value assigned to variable K in line 10. If you prefer 12 hour mode to 24 hour mode, change the 24 near to end of line 20 to 12.

Example: Set the alarm for 6:30 and the current time for 22:37:00.

Display	You Enter
>*>	ACLK
ALARM H?	6
M?	30
START H?	22
M?	37
S?	0 (enter this when the time is ripe.)
22.37.5.	
22.37.10.	
22.37.15.	
. . . a few winks later	
6.29.50.	
6.29.55.	
BEEP	
6.30.0.	
BEEP	
6.30.5.	
BEEP	
6.30.10.	
(twelve beeps between 6:30 and 6:31)	

Program length is 181 steps.

LISTING

```
10 "ACLK"CLEAR
   : K=.1415
   : INPUT"ALARM H?",I,"M?,N,"START H?",H,"M?",
   M,"S?",S
20 S=S+5
   : S=S*(S < 60)
```

```
   : M=M+(S=0)
   : M=M*(M < 60 )
   : H=H+(M=0)*(S=0)
   : H=H*(H < 24)
30 Y=Y+K
   : IF Y < 1 THEN 30
40 BEEP (H=I)*(M=N)
   : Y=Y-1
   : PAUSE H;M;S
   : GOTO 20
```

Pocket Watch

This program turns your TRS-80 pocket computer into a TRS-80 pocket watch! The time is briefly displayed once every five seconds, in a 24 hour mode. If you prefer a 12 hour mode, change the 24 near the end of line 20 to a 12.

The accuracy of your pocket watch is controlled by the value of variable K. Adjust the K=.1262 part of line 10, a little at a time, to adjust the speed of your clock.

Display	You Enter
> > >	CLK
H?	8
M?	59
S?	45 (enter this when the time is ripe.)
8.59.50	
8.59.55	
9.0.0.	
9.0.5.	
(etc.)	

Program length is 141 steps.

LISTING

```
10 "CLK"CLEAR$
   : K=.1262
   : INPUT"H?",H,"M?",M,"S?",S
20 S=S+5
   : S=S*(S < 60)
   : M=M+(S=0)
   : M=M*(M < 60)
   : H=H+(M=0)*(S=0)
   : H=H*(H < 24)
30 Y=Y+K
   : IF Y < 1 THEN 30
40 Y=Y-1
   : PAUSE H;M;S
   : GOTO 20
```

Polar To Rectangular

This program converts a point expressed in polar notation (R,A) to rectangular notation (X,Y). Either radian or degree mode is okay, and the conversion works nicely for all quadrants.

For example, convert R=2* √5, A=135 degrees to rectangular notation. Assume DEG mode is set. (Fig. 30)

Display	You Enter
>>>	PR
R?	2* √5
A?	135
−3.16227766 3.16227766	ENTER (− √10, + √10)
>>>	

For examples of use in other quadrants refer to Figures 29 through 32.

Program length is 45 steps.

LISTING

```
10 "PR"INPUT"R?",R,"A?",A
20 X=R*COS A
   : Y=R*SIN A
   : PRINT X,Y
   : GOTO 1
```

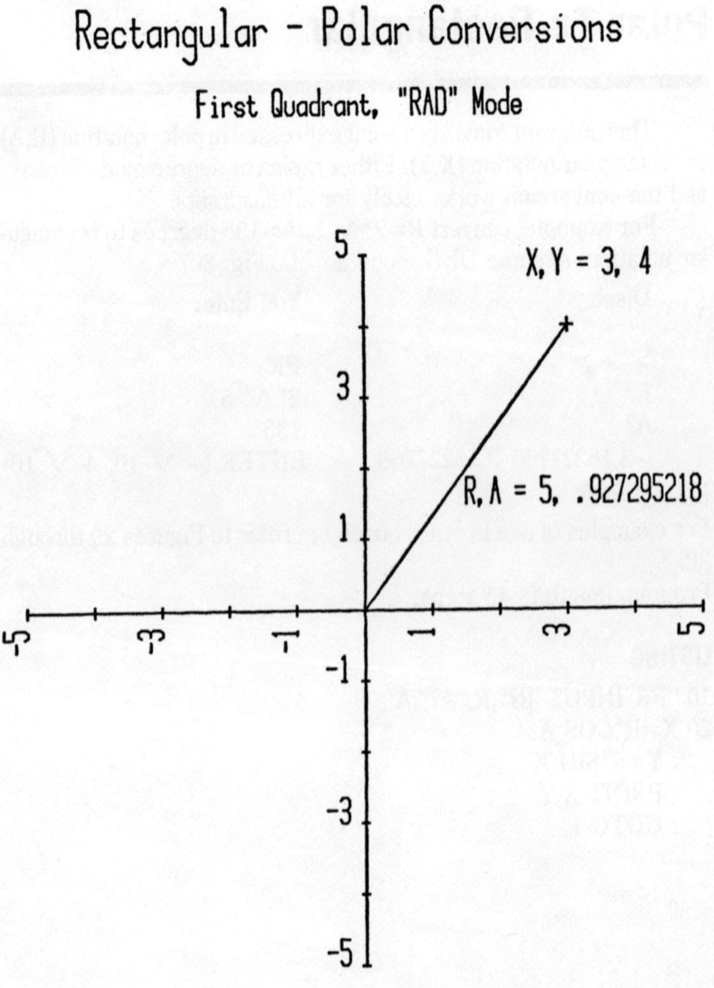

Rectangular - Polar Conversions
First Quadrant, "RAD" Mode
X, Y = 3, 4
R, A = 5, .927295218
5
3
1
-1
-3
-5
-5
-3
-1
1
3
5

Fig. 29.

Rectangular - Polar Conversions

Second Quadrant, "DEG" Mode

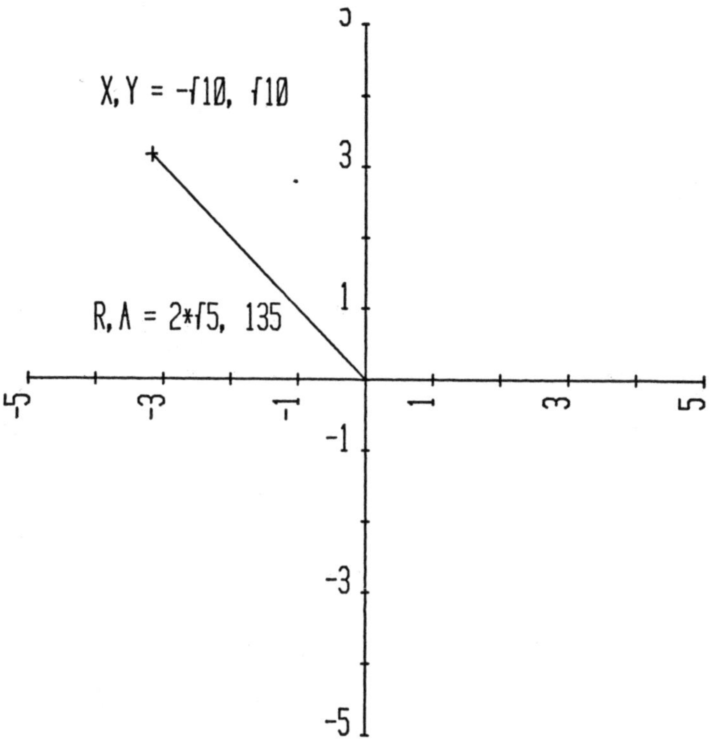

Fig. 30.

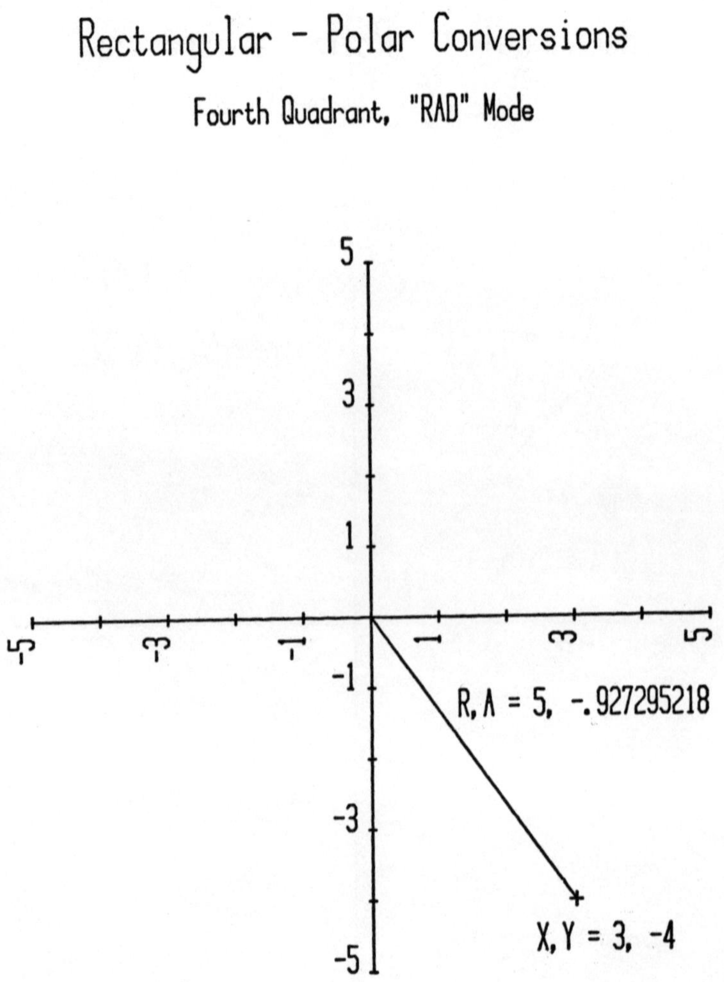

Rectangular - Polar Conversions
Fourth Quadrant, "RAD" Mode
5
3
1
-1
-3
-5
-5
-3
-1
1
3
5
R, A = 5, -.927295218
X, Y = 3, -4

Fig. 31.

Rectangular - Polar Conversions

Third Quadrant, "DEG" Mode

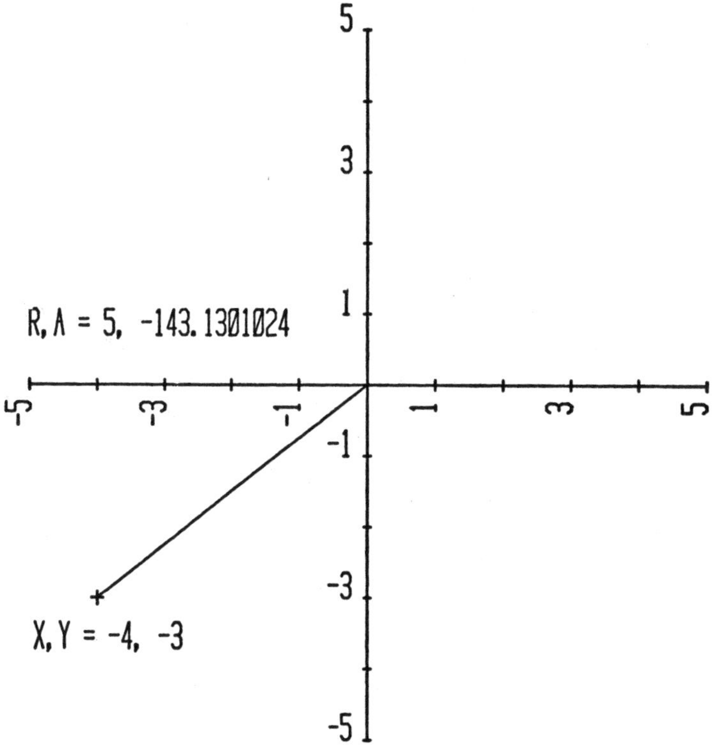

Fig. 32.

Polygon Area by Walkaround

This program computes the area of polygons of any shape. The X, Y coordinates of each vertex are needed for input. Enter these coordinates in the order they are encountered by walking around the perimeter in either direction. After the last pair of coordinates has been entered just press ENTER to complete the solution. For instance: What is the area of the polygon in Fig. 33?

Display	You Enter
> > >	PW
FIRST X?	.5
FIRST Y?	4
NEXT X?	8
NEXT Y?	2
NEXT X?	4.5
NEXT Y?	−1.5
NEXT X?	1
NEXT Y?	1
NEXT X?	.5
NEXT Y?	−2
NEXT X?	−1.5
NEXT Y?	.5
NEXT X?	ENTER
28.75 =AREA	ENTER
> > >	

Program length is 124 steps.

LISTING

```
10 "PW"S=0
   : INPUT"FIRST X?",T,"FIRST Y?",U
   : V=T
   : W=U
20 INPUT"NEXT X?",X,"NEXT Y?",Y
   : S=S+VY−XW
   : V=X
   : W=Y
   : GOTO 20
30 PRINT ABS((S+XU−TY) / 2); " =AREA"
   : GOTO 1
```

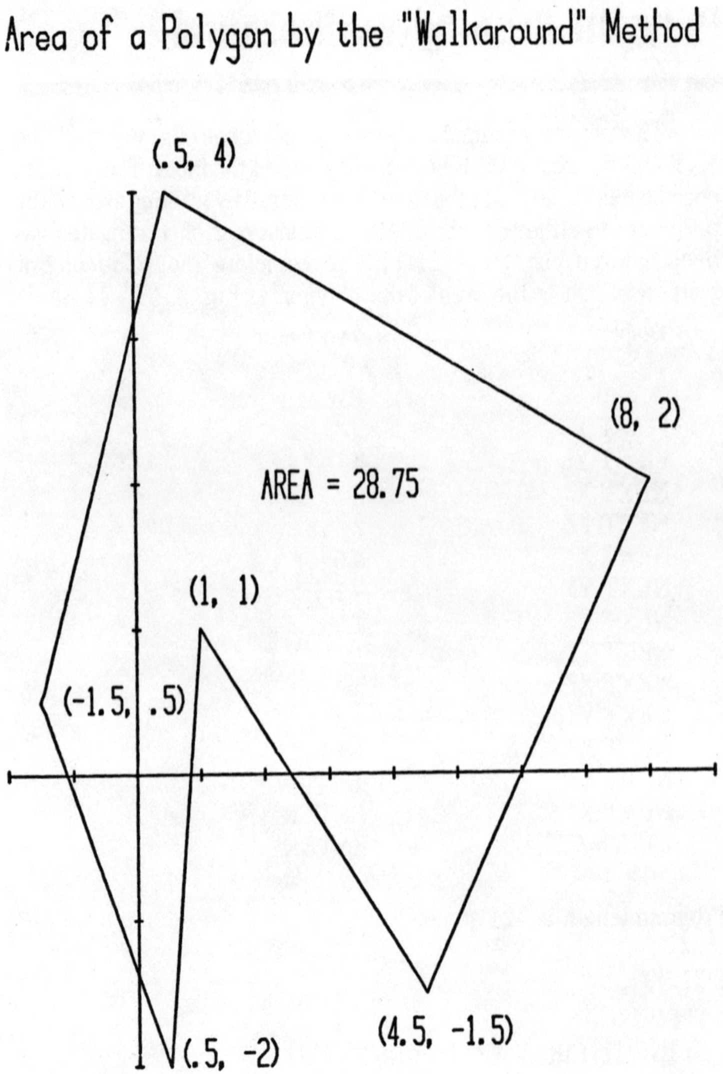
Area of a Polygon by the "Walkaround" Method
(.5, 4)
(8, 2)
AREA = 28.75
(1, 1)
(-1.5, .5)
(4.5, -1.5)
(.5, -2)

Fig. 33.

Polygons—Regular

This program computes seven facts about any regular polygon. You must input any two of the following four quantities. The number of sides, length of each side, radius of an inscribed circle, and radius of a circumscribed circle. Example: Describe a five sided regular polygon (pentagon) that just fits inside a circle with radius of 1. (Fig. 34)

Display	You Enter
>>>	POLY
# SIDES?	5
LEN SIDE?	ENTER
INSCRIBED RADIUS?	ENTER
CIRCUMSCRIBED RADIUS?	1
4.999999998 SIDES	ENTER
1.175570505 SIDE LEN	ENTER
.8090169942 INS RAD	ENTER
1. CIR RAD	ENTER
5.877852523 PERIMETER	ENTER
108. VERTEX ANGLE	ENTER
2.37764129 AREA	ENTER
>>>	

Program length is 372 steps.

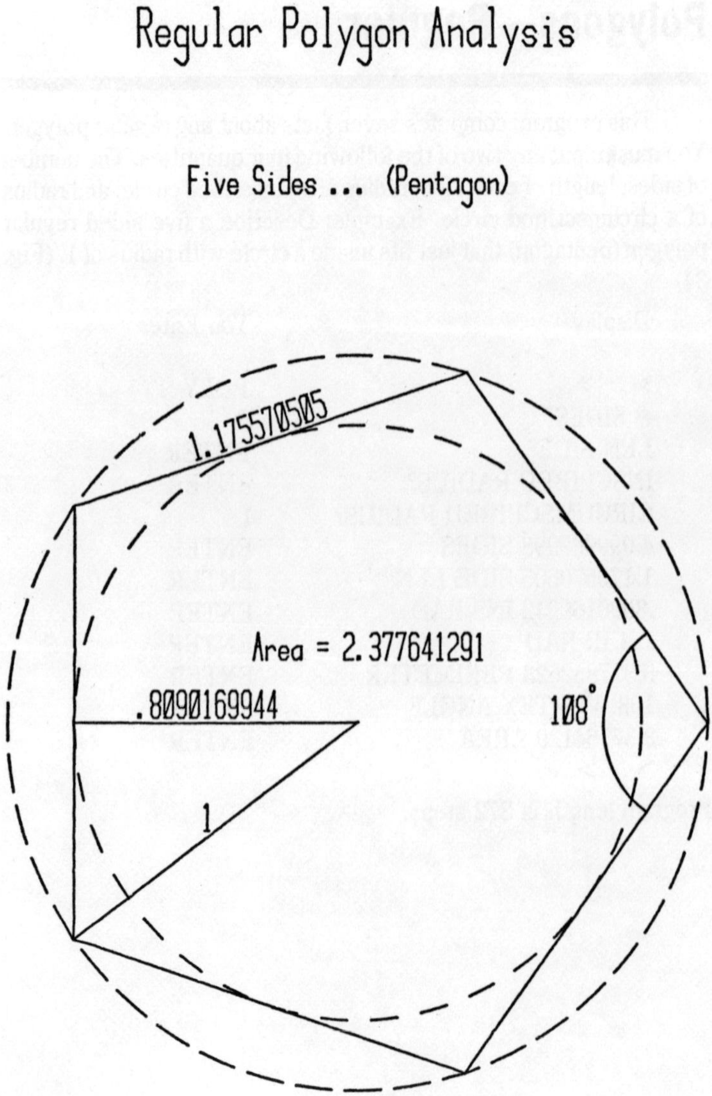
Regular Polygon Analysis
Five Sides ... (Pentagon)
1.1755705505
Area = 2.377641291
.8090169944
108°
1

Fig. 34.

LISTING

```
 10 "POLY"CLEAR
    : A=4*ATN 1
 20 INPUT"# SIDES?",N
 30 INPUT"LEN SIDE?",S
 40 IF NS=0 INPUT"INSCRIBED RADIUS?",I
 50 IF NS+SI+NI=0 INPUT"CIRCUMSCRIBED RADIUS?",R
 60 IF NS LET I=S / 2 / TAN (A / N)
 70 IF NI LET S=2I*TAN(A / N)
 80 IF SI LET N=A / ATN(S / 2I)
 90 IF NR LET S=2R*SIN(A / N)
100 IF SR LET N=A / ASN(S / 2R)
110 IF IR LET N=A / ACS(I / R)
120 IF NSI=0 THEN 60
130 A=A / N
    : PRINT N;" SIDES"
    : PRINT S;" SIDE LEN"
140 PRINT I;" INS RAD"
    : PRINT S / 2 / SIN A;" CIR RAD"
150 PRINT SN;" PERIMETER"
    : PRINT AN-2A;" VERTEX ANGLE"
160 PRINT NII*TAN A;" AREA"
    : GOTO 1
```

Prime Numbers

This program searches for prime numbers beginning with an integer of your choice. For instance: What are the first three primes greater than 100?

Display	You Enter
> > >	PRI
START N?	100
101. IS PRIME	ENTER
103. IS PRIME	ENTER
107. IS PRIME	ON
BREAK AT 30	

Program length is 100 steps.

LISTING

```
10 "PRI"INPUT"START N?",X
   : X=INT(X / 2)*2-1
20 X=X+2
   : Y=1
30 Y=Y+2
   : IF Y > √X PRINT X;" IS PRIME"
   : GOTO 20
40 Z=X / Y
   : GOTO 30-10*(Z=INT Z)
```

Quadratic Equations

This program finds the roots of any quadratic equation. A special output format will indicate if the roots are complex.

First example: (Fig. 35) What are the roots of X^2 + 4X +3 = 0?

Display	You Enter
>>>	QE
AX^2+BX+C=0 A?	1
B?	4
C?	3
−1. −3.	ENTER
>>>	

Second example: What are the roots of X^2 +2X +3 = 0?

Display	You Enter
>>>	QE
AX^2+BX + C=0 A?	1
B?	2
C?	3
COMPLEX RESULT FOLLOWS	ENTER
REAL= −1.	ENTER
+ / − (I) = 1.414213562	ENTER
>>>	

Program length is 154 steps.

LISTING

```
10 "QE"INPUT"AX^2+BX+C=0 A?",A,"B?",B,"C?",C
20 D=(BB−4AC) / 4 / AA
   : E=−B / 2 / A
   : F= √ABS D
30 IF D LET S=E−F,
   : PRINT E+F,S
   : GOTO 1
40 PRINT"COMPLEX RESULT FOLLOWS"
   : PRINT" REAL= ";E
   : PRINT"+ / − (I) = ";F
   : GOTO 1
```

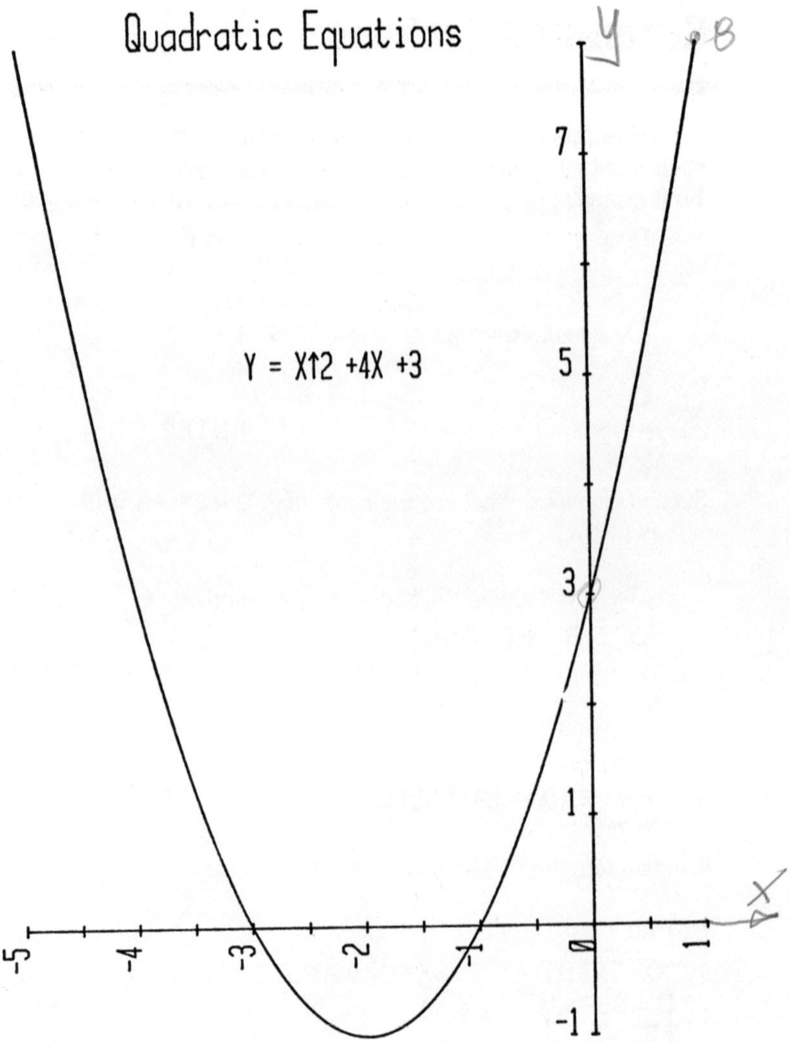

Fig. 35.

x	$y=x^2+4x+3$
3	$y=3^2+4\times3+3=24$
2	$y=4+8+3=15$
1	$y=1+4+3=8$
0	$y=0+0+3=3$
-1	$y=1-4+3=0$
-2	$y=4-8+3=-1$
-3	$y=9-12+3=0$
-4	$y=12-16+3=-1$

Radioisotope Activity

This program flexibly answers questions about radioisotope activity. You input any three quantities and the fourth is computed. The four quantities are the starting activity, half-life, elapsed time, and the final activity. When asked to input the unknown, just press ENTER. Example: On August 27 an isotope of chromium has an activity of 127 microcuries. The half-life is known to be 667.2 hours. What was the activity on August 3? (Fig. 36)

Display	You Enter	
>>>	RAD	
START ACTIVITY?	ENTER	
HALF-LIFE?	667.2	(hours)
ELAPSED TIME?	(27–3)*24	(hours)
FINAL ACTIVITY?	127	
ST ACT= 231.0392317	ENTER	
>>>		

Program length is 242 steps.

LISTING

```
10 "RAD"CLEAR
   : INPUT"START ACTIVITY?",A
20 INPUT"HALF-LIFE?",H
30 INPUT"ELAPSED TIME?",T
40 IF AHT=0 INPUT"FINAL ACTIVITY?",B
50 IF A=0 LET A=B /  .5^(T / H)
   : PRINT"ST ACT= ";A
60 IF H=0 LET H=T*LN .5 / LN(B / A)
   : PRINT"HALFLF= ";H
70 IF T=0 LET T=H*LN(B / A) / LN .5
   : PRINT"TIME= ";T
80 IF B=0 LET B=A*.5^(T / H)
   : PRINT"END ACT= ";B
90 GOTO 1
```

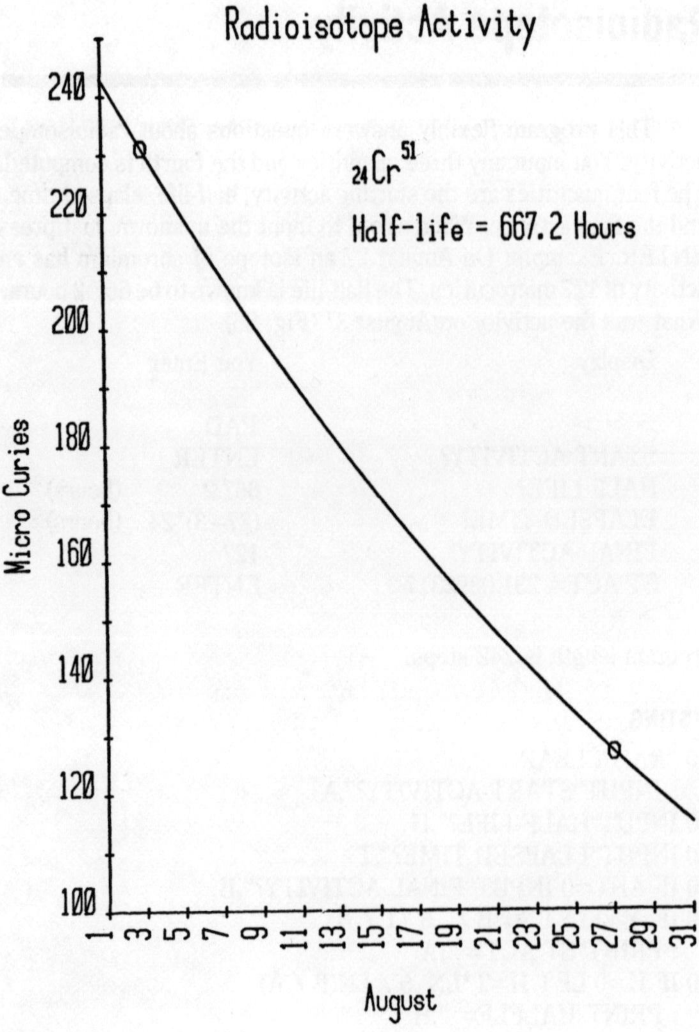

Radioisotope Activity
24Cr51
Half-life = 667.2 Hours
Micro Curies
240
220
200
180
160
140
120
100
1 3 5 7 9 11 13 15 17 19 21 23 25 27 29 31
August

Fig. 36.

Random Numbers—Exponential Distribution

This program generates pseudorandom numbers with an exponential distribution. You input the mean. Figure 37 is a histogram of 10,000 random numbers in an exponential distribution with mean of 50. The algorithm of this program was used to generate the histogram.

Example: Generate five random numbers from an exponential distribution with a mean of 50.

Display	You Enter
>>>	RNDE
MEAN?	50
65.07705826	ENTER
41.35034278	ENTER
84.1209901	ENTER
33.93044871	ENTER
2.996731433	ON
>>>	

Program length is 48 steps.

LISTING

```
10 "RNDE"INPUT"MEAN? ";M
20 R=π+997R
   : R=R-INT R
   : PRINT -M*LN R
   : GOTO 20
```

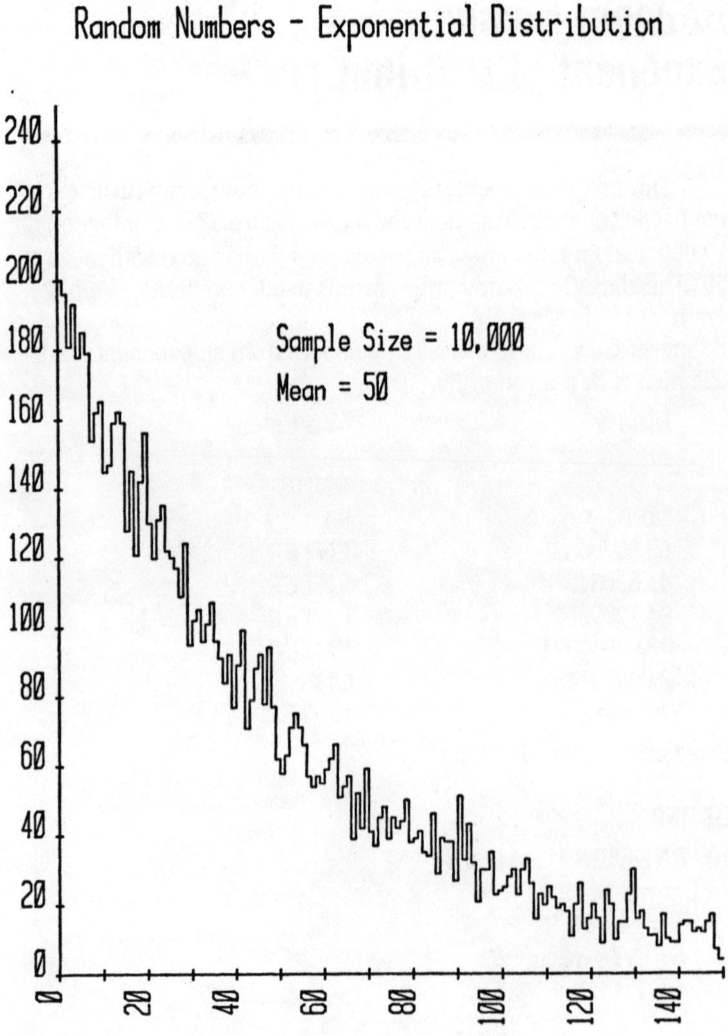
Random Numbers - Exponential Distribution
Sample Size = 10,000
Mean = 50
240
220
200
180
160
140
120
100
80
60
40
20
0
0
20
40
60
80
100
120
140
Fig. 37.

Random Numbers—Integers from I to J

This program generates pseudorandom integers in a range of your choice. Figure 38 is a histogram of 10,000 integers generated by this algorithm.

Example: Generate five random integers in the range 0 to 9.

Display	You Enter
>>>	RNDI
(I TO J) I?	0
J?	9
0	ENTER
8	ENTER
8	ENTER
6	ENTER
4	ON
BREAK AT 20	

Program length is 68 steps.

LISTING

```
10 "RNDI"INPUT"(I TO J) I?",I,"J?", J
20 R= π + 997R
   : R=R–INT R
   : PRINT I+INT(RJ–RI+R)
   : GOTO 20
```

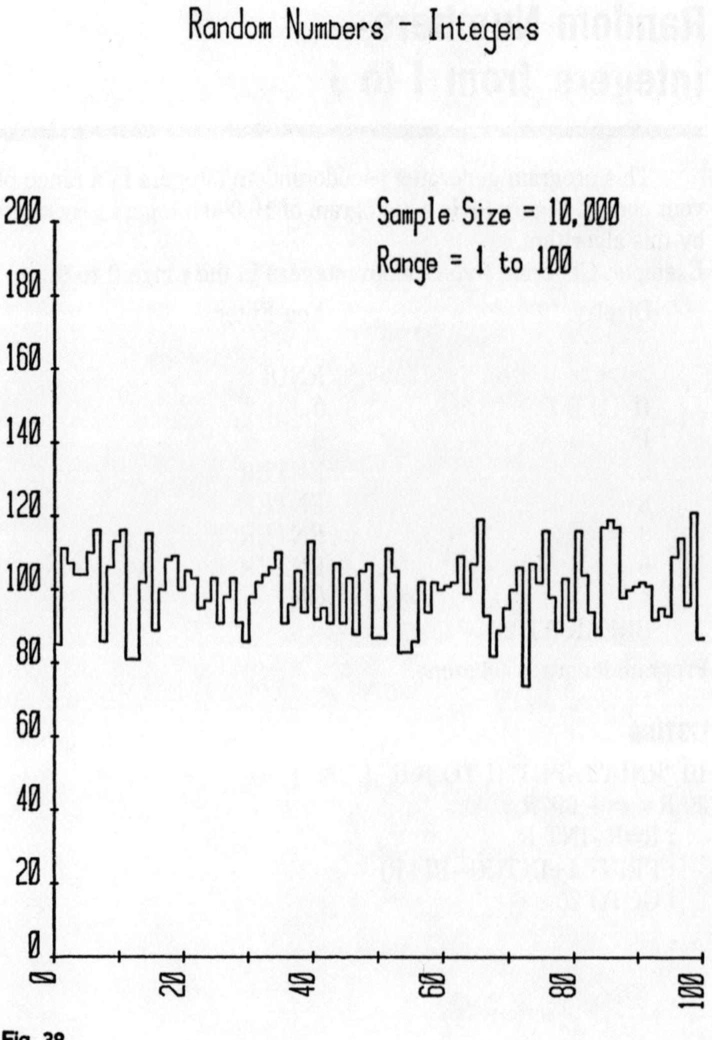
Random Numbers - Integers
Sample Size = 10,000
Range = 1 to 100
200
180
160
140
120
100
80
60
40
20
0
0
20
40
60
80
100

Fig. 38.

Random Numbers—Normal Distribution

This program generates pseudorandom numbers in the bell-shaped normal distribution. You control the shape and range of the distribution by inputting the mean and standard deviation.

Example: Generate five normally distributed random numbers with mean of 50 and standard deviation of 20. (Fig. 39)

Display	You Enter
>>>	RNDN
MEAN?	50
ST DEV?	20
40.93779009	ENTER
73.62533292	ENTER
34.21830622	ENTER
180.7990033	ENTER
36.72625559	ON
BREAK AT 30	

Program length is 117 steps.

LISTING

```
10 "RNDN"INPUT"MEAN?",M,"ST DEV?",D
20 GOSUB 40
   : S=R
   : GOSUB 40
   : A=2S-1
   : B=2R-1
   : B=AA+BB
   : IF 1 < B THEN 20
30 PRINT DA* √(-2 * LN B / B) + M
   : GOTO 20
40 R= π + 997R
   : R=R-INT R
   : RETURN
```

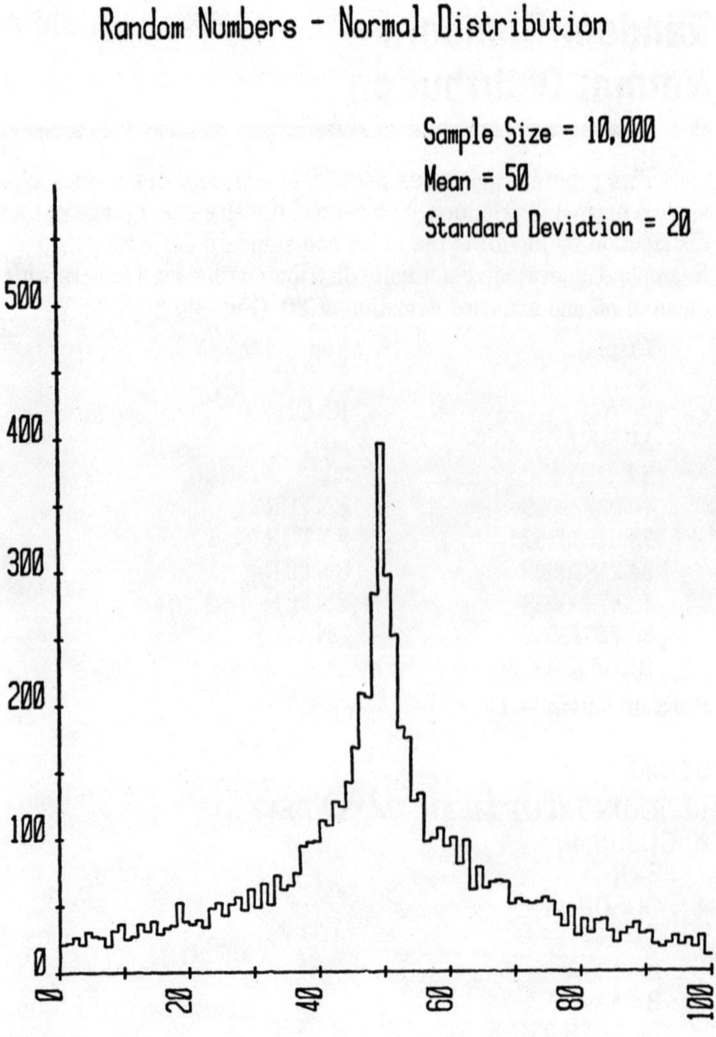
Random Numbers - Normal Distribution
Sample Size = 10,000
Mean = 50
Standard Deviation = 20
500
400
300
200
100
0
0
20
40
60
80
100

Fig. 39.

Random Numbers—Reals from A to B

This program generates pseudorandom real numbers in a range you define. The sequence is determined by the variable R. To force the same sequence to repeat, load R with the same value each time you run the program. In Fig. 40, random real numbers in the range 0 to 100 were generated in pairs with this program and plotted as X,Y points.

Example: Generate five random real numbers in the range π to 2π.

Display	You Enter
>>>	RNDR
(A to B) A?	π
B?	2π
3.586420183	ENTER
4.114901098	ENTER
3.222807851	ENTER,
6.018153796	ENTER
3.243785836	ON
BREAK AT 20	

Program length is 63 steps.

LISTING

```
10 "RNDR"INPUT"(A TO B) A?",A,"B?",B
20 R= π + 997R
   : R=R-INT R
   : PRINT A+RB-RA
   : GOTO 20
```

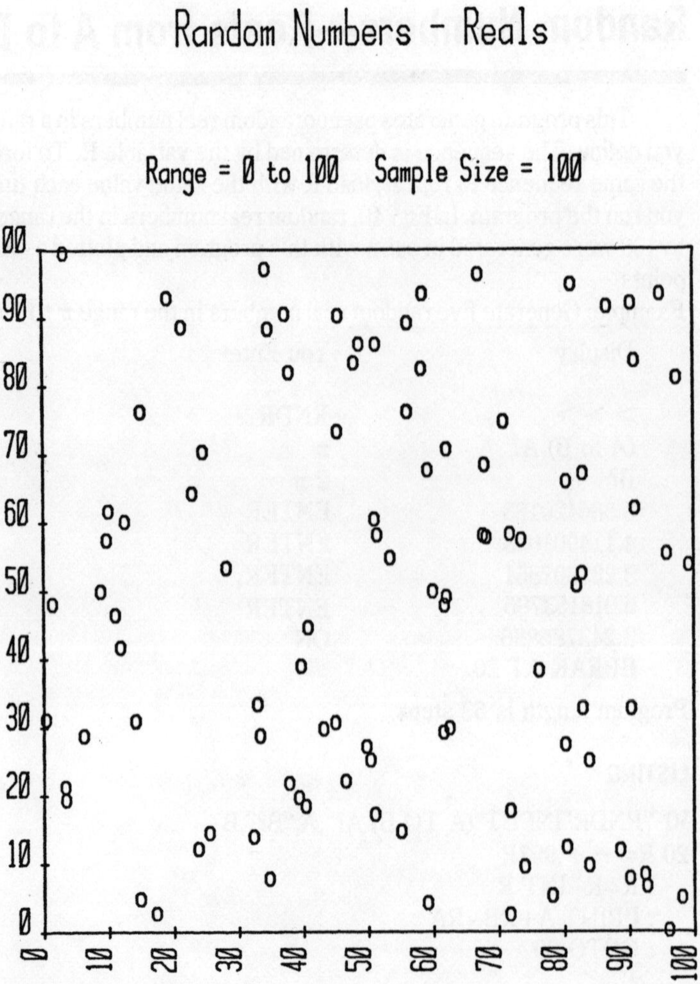
Random Numbers - Reals
Range = 0 to 100 Sample Size = 100
0
10
20
30
40
50
60
70
80
90
100

Fig. 40.

Rectangular to Polar

This program converts a point expressed in rectangular notation (X,Y) to polar notation (R,A). Either radian or degree mode is ok, and the conversion works nicely for all quadrants. For example: Convert X=3, Y=4 to polar notation. Assume RAD mode is set.

Display	You Enter
>>>	RP
X?	3
Y?	4
5. 0.927295218	ENTER (length of 5 at .927295218 radians)
>>>	

Program length is 66 steps.

LISTING

```
10 "RP"INPUT"X?",X,"Y?",Y
20 R=√(XX+YY)
   : A=ACS(X / R)
   : A=A*SGN Y+A*(Y=0)
   : PRINT R,A
   : GOTO 1
```

Relativity

This program computes the dilation or contraction of length, time, or mass for velocities approaching the velocity of light.

You must input two quantities, the first being either velocity or gamma (which is a direct function of velocity). If the velocity is known as a fraction of the velocity of light then multiply by C while entering the value. (See the first example).

The second quantity to be entered is either length, time, or mass. Just press ENTER to bypass the unknown quantities.

The first pair of answers give new measurements for the entered data. On the left is the conversion from the rest frame to the moving frame. On the right is the conversion from the moving frame to the rest frame. Follow the examples to see this more clearly. First example: A mass of 10 kg is accelerated to 95% of the velocity of light. What is its mass as measured from the rest frame?

Display	You Enter
>>>	REL
VEL?	.95C
LEN?	ENTER
TIME?	ENTER
MASS?	10
32.02563074 3.122499001	ENTER
VEL= 284787200.	ENTER
V / C= 0.95	ENTER
GAMMA= 3.202563074	ENTER
>>>	

Answer is approximately 32 kg. If its mass at .95C is 10 kg., its rest mass is about 3 kg.

Second example: If gamma is 5, what is the velocity? Also, if an object at this velocity measures 7 meters in length, what will its length be at rest?

Display	You Enter
>>>	REL
VEL?	ENTER
GAMMA?	5
LEN?	7
1.4 35.	ENTER

```
VEL= 293719294.9            ENTER
V / C= .9797958973          ENTER
GAMMA= 5.                   ENTER
>>>
```

The velocity is approximately 89% of the velocity of light, and the object will measure 35 meters at rest.
Program length is 206 steps.

LISTING

```
10 "REL"C=2.99776 E8
20 INPUT"VEL?",V
   : G=1 / √(1-VV / CC)
   : GOTO 40
30 INPUT"GAMMA?",G
   : V= √(CC-CC / GG)
40 B=V / C
   : INPUT"LEN?",L
   : Y=LG
   : PRINT L / G,Y
   : GOTO 70
50 INPUT"TIME?",T
   : Y=T / G
   : PRINT TG,Y
   : GOTO 70
60 INPUT"MASS?",M
   : Y=M / G
   : PRINT MG,Y
70 PRINT"VEL= ";V
   : PRINT"V / C= ";B
   : PRINT"GAMMA= ";G
   : GOTO 1
```

Simultaneous Equations—Size Two

This program solves two equations of two unknowns. Example:

X +2Y = −3
4X +3Y = 0

Display	You Enter
> > >	SE2
?	1
?	2
?	−3
?	4
?	3
?	0
1.8 −2.4	ENTER
> > >	

Program length is 56 steps.

LISTING

```
10 "SE2"INPUT U,V,W,X,Y,Z
   : D=UY-VX
   : F=(UZ-WX) / D
   : PRINT (WY-VZ) / D,F
   : GOTO 1
```

Simultaneous Equations—Size Three

This program solves three equations of three unknowns. Example:

3X +2Y −4Z = 7
X −3Y +2Z = 5
Y + 5Z = 20

Display	You Enter
> > >	SE3
BEEP	
EQ # 1.	
?	3
?	2
?	−4
?	7
BEEP	
EQ # 2.	
?	1
?	−3
?	2
?	5
BEEP	
EQ # 3	
?	0
?	1
?	5
?	20
1)= 5.369230769	ENTER
2)= 2.4615384562	ENTER
3) 3.507692308	ENTER
> > >	

Program length is 208 steps.

LISTING

```
10 "SE3"FOR I=1 TO 3
   : BEEP 1
   : PAUSE"EQ # ";I
   : FOR J=1 TO 4
```

```
   : INPUT A(4I+J+10)
   : NEXT J
   : NEXT I
20 D=OTY+PUW+QSX-QTW-PSY-OUX
   : A=(RTY+PUZ+QVX-QTZ-PVY-RUX) / D
30 B=(OVY+RUW+QSZ-QVW-RSY-OUZ) / D
   : C=(OTZ+PVW+RSX-RTW-PSZ-OVX) / D
40 PRINT"1)= ";A
   : PRINT"2)= ";B
   : PRINT"3)= ";C
   : GOTO 1
```

Simultaneous Equations—Flexible Size

This program solves up to roughly eleven simultaneous equations, depending on available memory. However, as the number of equations / unknowns increases, the computation time becomes excessive.

While inputting the coefficients you may want to verify where you're at. Just press ENTER and you'll be told the equation number and the coefficient number (or constant) that is to be entered. Example: (Fig. 41) A pile of 18 coins is comprised of pennies, nickels, dimes, and quarters. There is $.70 in nickels and dimes, $2.00 in dimes and quarters, and $2.23 altogether. How many coins of each type?

Display	You Enter
>>>	SIEQ
# EQUATIONS?	4
?	1
?	1
?	1
?	1
?	18
?	ENTER
EQ #2. COEF#1.	
?	1
?	5
?	10
?	25
?	ENTER
EQ #2. CONST5.	
?	223
?	0
?	5
?	10
?	0
?	70
?	0
?	0
?	10

```
?                                25
?                                200
BEEP
1. ) = 3.                        ENTER
2. ) = 4.                        ENTER
3. ) = 5.                        ENTER
4. ) = 6.                        ENTER
> > >
```

There are 3 pennies, 4 nickels, 5 dimes, and 6 quarters.
Program length is 457 steps.

LISTING

```
 10 "SIEQ"INPUT"# EQUATIONS?",A
    : A(AA+A+7)=0
    : FOR F=1 TO A
    : FOR E=1 TO A+1
 20 : INPUT A(FA+F+E−A+6)
    · NEXT E
    : NEXT F
    : GOTO 50
 30 D$=" COEF#"
    : IF E=A+1 LET D$=" CONST"
 40 PAUSE"EQ #";F;D$;E
    : GOTO 20
 50 FOR F=1 TO A
    : E=F
 60 IF ABS A(EA+E+F−A+6) GOTO 90
 70 E=E+1
    : IF E < = A THEN 60
 80 PRINT"UNSOLVABLE"
    : GOTO 1
 90 FOR G=1 TO A+1
    : B=FA+F+G−A+6
    : C=EA+E+G−A+6
      D=A(B)
    · A(B)=A(C)
      A(C)=D
    : NEXT G
100 B=A(FA+2F−A+6)
    : FOR G=1 TO A+1
    : C=FA+F+G−A+6
```

```
    : A(C)=A(C) / B
    : NEXT G
110 FOR E=1 TO A
    : IF E=F THEN 130
120 B=A(EA+E+F-A+6)
    : FOR G=1 TO A+1
    : C=EA+E+G-A+6
    : A(C)=A(C)-BA(FA+F+G-A+6)
    : NEXT G
130 NEXT E
    : NEXT F
    : BEEP 1
    FOR E=1 TO A
    : B=A(EA+E+7)
140 PRINT E;")= ";B
    : NEXT E
    : GOTO 1
```

Simultaneous Equations - Flexible Size

P - Pennies
N - Nickels
D - Dimes
Q - Quarters

A) Total of 18 coins.

B) $2.23 total value.

C) $2.ØØ worth of dimes and quarters.

D) $Ø.7Ø worth of nickels and dimes.

P +	N +	D +	Q	=	18
P +	5N +	1ØD +	25Q	=	223
	5N +	1ØD		=	7Ø
		1ØD +	25Q	=	2ØØ

Solution ...

3 Pennies 4 Nickels 5 Dimes 6 Quarters

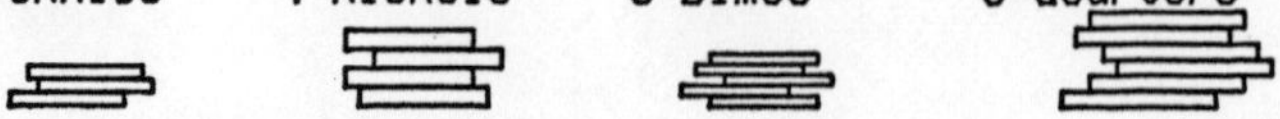

Fig. 41.

Spherical Triangles

This collection of six programs computes the sides and angles of spherical triangles. (Fig. 42) Input the known values in the order they're encountered while walking around your triangle. For instance, if you know two sides and the included angle, use program SAS. Enter a side, the angle, then the other side. All of the sides and angles will be displayed after the unknowns are computed.

Either degree or radian mode is ok. But make sure that all angles and sides are expressed in the current units.

There may be two correct solutions when using either "SSA" or "AAS". If so, both sets of correct solutions will be displayed, separated by a beep. Example: Given sides of 20 and 40 units, and an included angle of 30 degrees, find the other sides and angles.

Display		You Enter
>>>		SAS
?		20
?		30
?		40
SIDE, OPP ANGLE		ENTER
20.	24.39244173	ENTER
24.46162718	30.	ENTER
40.	129.0899896	ENTER
>>>		

Program length is 542 steps.

LISTING

```
 10 "SSS"GOSUB 130
    : J=-1
    : GOSUB 20
    : GOTO 160
 20 D=ACS((COS A+J*COS B*COS C) / SIN B / SIN C)
 30 E=ACS((COS B+J*COS A*COS C) / SIN A / SIN C)
 40 F=ACS ((COS C+J*COS A*COS B) / SIN A / SIN B)
    : RETURN
 50 "AAA"GOSUB 130
 60 J=1
    : GOSUB 20
    : FOR Z=1 TO 3
    : T=A(Z)
    : A(Z)=A(Z+3)
    : A(Z+3)=T
    : NEXT Z
    : GOTO 160
 70 "SAS"GOSUB 130
    : B=ACS(COS B*SIN A*SIN C+COS A*COS C)
    : J=-1
    : GOSUB 20
    : GOTO 160
 80 "ASA"GOSUB 130
    : B=ACS(COS B*SIN A*SIN C-COS A*COS C)
    : GOTO 60
 90 "SSA"GOSUB 130
    : D=C
    : E=ASN(SIN B*SIN D / SIN A)
100 GOSUB 140
    : G=(A < B)*I
    : GOTO 160
110 "AAS"GOSUB 130
    : D=A
    : E=B
    : A=C
    : B=ASN(SIN E*SIN A / SIN D)
120 GOSUB 140
    : H=(D < E)*I
    : GOTO 160
130 INPUT A,B,C
    : I=1
```

```
    : G=0
    : H=0
    : RETURN
140 C=2*ATN(SIN((D+E) / 2)*TAN((A-B)
    / 2) / SIN((D-E) / 2))
150 F=ACS((COS C-COS A*COS B) / SIN A / SIN B
    :RETURN
160 PRINT"SIDE, OPP ANGLE"
    : PRINT A,D
    : PRINT B,E
    : PRINT C,F
170 IF G BEEP 1
    : E=ACS-COS E
    : I=0
    : GOTO 100
180 IF H BEEP 1
    : B=ACS-COS B
    : I=0
    : GOTO 120
190 GOTO 1
```

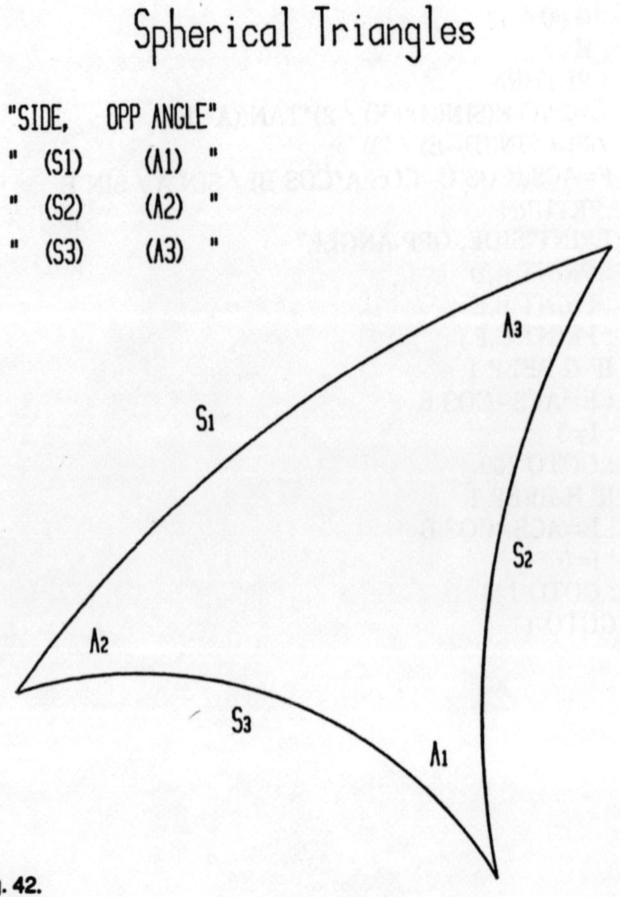

Spherical Triangles
"SIDE, OPP ANGLE"
" (S1) (A1) "
" (S2) (A2) "
" (S3) (A3) "
A3
S1
S2
A2
S3
A1

Fig. 42.

Temperature Conversions

This program converts temperatures between the Celsius and Fahrenheit scales. Two values are displayed as results. The left value assumes conversion from F to C, the right value assumes conversion from C to F. Notice how the order of C and F in the program label "CF" relates to the order of the answers. For instance: Convert 32°F to C, and 100°C to F.

Display	You Enter	
>>>	CF	
?	32	
0. 89.6	ENTER	(Answer is on left.)
>>>	CF	
?	100	
37.77777778 212.	ENTER	(Answer is on right.)
>>>		

Program length is 46 steps.

LISTING

```
10 "CF"INPUT X
   : Y=40
   : Z=1.8
   : F=ZX+ZY-Y
   : PRINT (X+Y) / Z-Y, F
   : GOTO 1
```

Triangle Analysis

"SSA" - Two Correct Solutions

S ... 4

S ... 5

A ... 45°

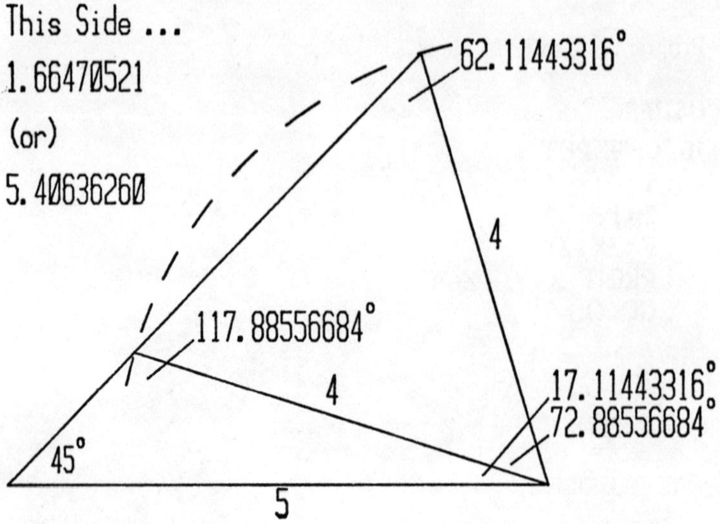

Fig. 43.

Triangle Analysis

This collection of five programs computes the angles, sides, and area of any triangle. You input values for three of the sides or angles and all results are displayed. The program to use depends on the known data.

ASA—If you know two angles and the included side.
SSS—If you know three sides.
SAA—If you know one side, the opposite angle, and one other angle.
SAS—If you know two sides and the included angle.
SSA—If you know two sides and an angle other than the included angle.

Values are entered in the same order that the program label indicates. Walk around the triangle and enter the known values as they are encountered. A side, the angle, then another side for SAS for instance. When solving the SSA case it sometimes is possible to arrive at two different valid solutions. This program automatically displays results for both solutions. (Fig. 43) while either degree or radian mode may be used, make sure that your angles are expressed in the current mode.

Example: Completely describe a triangle that has sides of 3 and 4 and an included angle of 90 degrees. (Fig. 44)

Display	You Enter
>>>	SAS
?	3
?	90
?	4
SIDE, OPP ANGLE	ENTER
3. 36.86989766	ENTER
4. 53.13010237	ENTER
5. 89.99999997	ENTER
AREA= 6.	ENTER
>>>	

Program length is 401 steps.

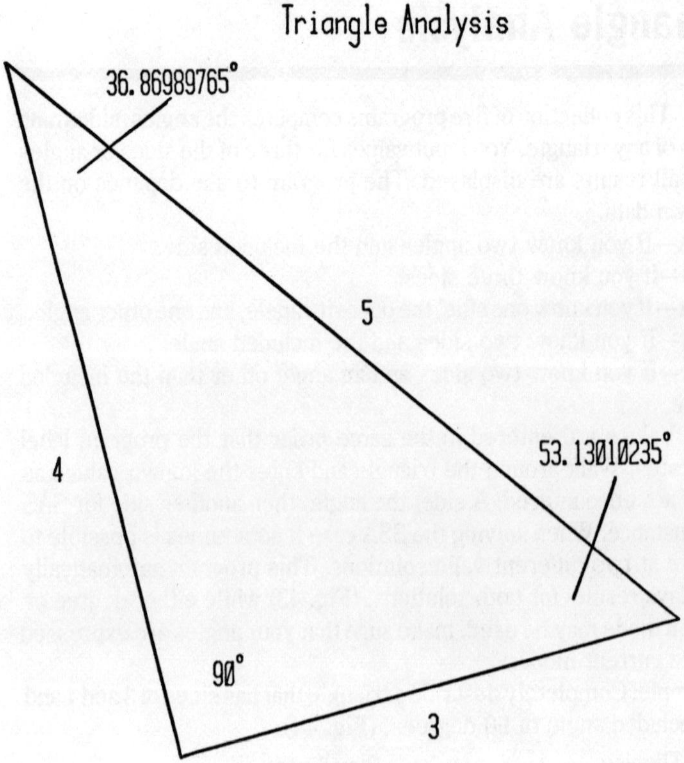

Fig. 44.

LISTING

```
 10 "ASA"GOSUB 200
    : E=A
    : A=B
    : F=C
 20 D=ACS-COS (E+F)
    : B=A*SIN E / SIN D
    : C=A*COS E+B*COS D
    : GOTO 300
 30 "SSS"GOSUB 200
 40 J=(A+B+C) / 2
    : E=2*ACS √( (JJ-JB) / AC)
    : D=2*ACS √( (JJ-JA) / BC)
 50 F=ACS-COS (D+E)
    : GOTO 300
 60 "SAA"GOSUB 200
    : F=B
    : D=C
    : E=ACS-COS(D+F)
    : GOTO 20
 70 "SAS"GOSUB 200
    : F=B
    : B=C
    : C= √(AA+BB-2AB*COS F)
    : GOTO 40
 80 "SSA"GOSUB 200
    : D=C
    : E=ASN (SIN D*B / A)
    : G=ACS-COS E
 90 H=ACS-COS(D+G)
    :F=ACS-COS(D+E)
    : I=(B > A)*COS D
    : GOTO 20
200 I=0
    : INPUT A,B,C
    : RETURN
300 PRINT"SIDE, OPP ANGLE"
    : PRINT A,D
    : PRINT B,E
    : PRINT C,F
310 K=AB*SIN F / 2
    : PRINT"AREA= ";K
```

```
320 IF I BEEP 1
    : E=G
    : F=H
    : I=0
    : GOTO 20
330 GOTO 1
```

Triangles—In Space

This program computes the angles, sides, and area of a triangle defined by three points in space (X,Y,Z). See Fig. 45.
For example: Describe the triangle formed by connecting the following three points in space.

(0,1,3) (3,0,5) (4,2,2)

Display	You Enter
>>>	T3D
X?	0
Y?	1
Z?	3
X?	3
Y?	0
Z?	5
X?	4
Y?	2
Z?	2
SIDE, OPP ANGLE	ENTER
3.741657387 55.46241618	ENTER
3.741657387 55.46241618	ENTER
4.242640687 69.07516764	ENTER
AREA= 6.538348419	ENTER
>>>	

Program length is 302 steps.

LISTING

```
10 "T3D"FOR Z=1 TO 3
   : W=3Z-2
   : X=W+1
   : Y=3Z
   : INPUT"X?",A(W), "Y?",A(X),"Z?",A(Y)
   : NEXT Z
20 R=AA+BB+CC
   : S=DD+EE+FF
   : T=GG+HH+II
30 J= √(R+S-2*(AD+BE+CF))
40 K= √(S+T-2*(DG+EH+FI))
50 L= √(T+R-2*(GA+HB+IC))
```

```
60 M=(J+K+L) / 2
   : O=2*ACS √ ((MM−MK) / JL)
70 N=2*ACS √ ((MM−MJ) / KL)
   : PC=ACS−COS (N+0)
80 PRINT"SIDE, OPP ANGLE"
   : PRINT J,N
   : PRINT K,O
   : PRINT L,P
90 Q=JK*SIN P / 2
   : PRINT"AREA= ";Q
   : GOTO 1
```

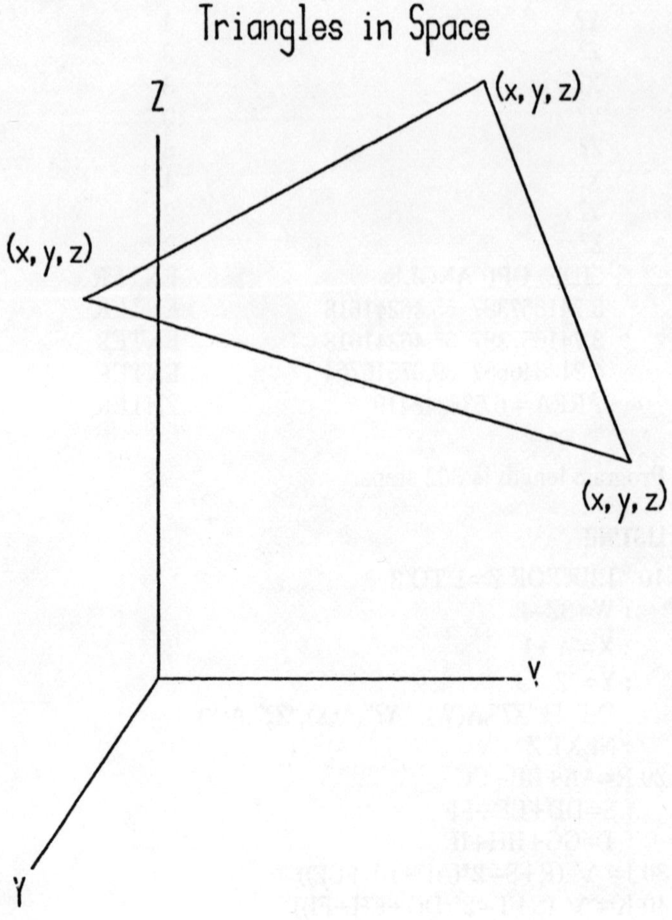

Fig. 45.

Vectors

This program simplifies vector computations by providing nine vector analysis functions. The programs are designed for three dimensional vectors, but two dimensional vectors can be analyzed by entering zero for the Z components. The nine functions are:

V+—Vector addition. (Fig. 46)
V-—Vector subtraction. (Fig. 47)
VC—Cross product of two vectors. (Fig. 48)
VT—Angle between two sectors "THETA".
VD—Dot product of two vectors. (Fig. 49)
VM—Magnitude of a vector.
VU—Unit vector in direction of a given vector. (Fig. 50)
VK—Vector multiplied by a scalar.
STP—Scalar triple product. (Fig. 51)

A sample problem for each function will help clarify their use.

V+—Add 3i + 4j – 5k to 2j + 7k.

Display	You Enter
>>>	V+
I1?	3
J1?	4
K1?	–5
I2?	0
J2?	2
K2?	7
I= 3.	ENTER
J= 6.	ENTER
K= 2.	ENTER
>>>	

Answer is 3i +6j +2k.

V-—Subtract 2i + k from 3i +j +k.

Display	You Enter
>>>	V-
I1?	3
J1?	1
K1?	1
I2?	2
J2?	0
K2?	1

I= 1.	ENTER
J= 1.	ENTER
K= 0.	ENTER
>>>	

Answer is i +j.

VC—What is the cross product of 3i + 4j and j −k?

Display	You Enter
>>>	VC
I1?	3
J1?	4
K1?	0
I2?	0
J2?	1
K2?	−1
I= −4.	ENTER
J= 3.	ENTER
K= 3.	ENTER
>>>	

Answer is −4i +3j +3k.

VT What is the angle, theta, between 3i + 4j + 12k and i + j −k? Assume that degree mode is set.

Display	You Enter
>>>	VT
I1?	3
J1?	4
K1?	12
I2?	1
J2?	1
K2?	−1
THETA= 102.8299261	ENTER
>>>	

VD—What is the dot product of 3i+4j +12k and i +j −k?

Display	You Enter
>>>	VD
I1?	3
J1?	4
K1?	12
I2?	1

J2?	1
K2?	−1
DOT= −5.	ENTER
> > >	

Answer is −5. (Scalar result).

VM—What is the magnitude of the vector 3i +4j −12k?

Display	You Enter
> > >	VM
I?	3
J?	4
K?	−12
MAG= 13.	ENTER
> > >	

Answer is 13 units magnitude.

VU—What is the unit vector in the direction of 3i +4j −12k?

Display	You Enter
> > >	VU
I?	3
J?	4
K?	−12
I= 2.307692308 *E*−01	ENTER
J= 3.076923077 *E*−01	ENTER
J=−9.230769231 *E*−01	ENTER
> > >	

Answer is approximately .231i +.308j −.923k

VK—Multiply the vector 2i +3j by the scalar 7.

Display	You Enter
> > >	VK
I?	2
J?	3
K?	0
SCALAR K?	7
I= 14.	ENTER
J= 21.	ENTER
K= 0.	ENTER
> > >	

Answer is 14i +21j.

STP—What is the scalar triple product of these three vectors?

$$\begin{array}{c} i + 2j \\ 3i - 2j - k \\ i + 4j + 3k \end{array}$$

Display	You Enter
> > >	STP
I1?	1
J1?	2
K1?	0
I2?	3
J2?	−2
K2?	−1
I3?	1
J3?	4
K3?	3
STP= −22.	ENTER
> > >	

Answer is −22. (scalar result).
Program length is 565 steps.

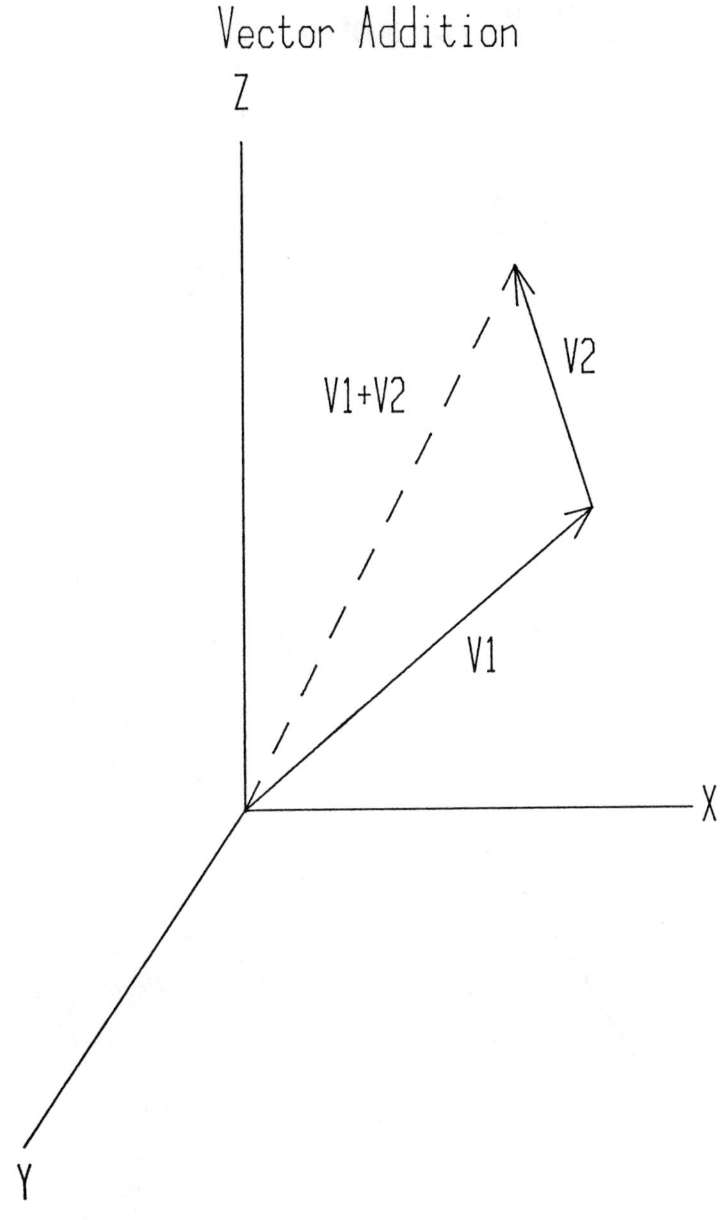

Fig. 46.

Vector Subtraction

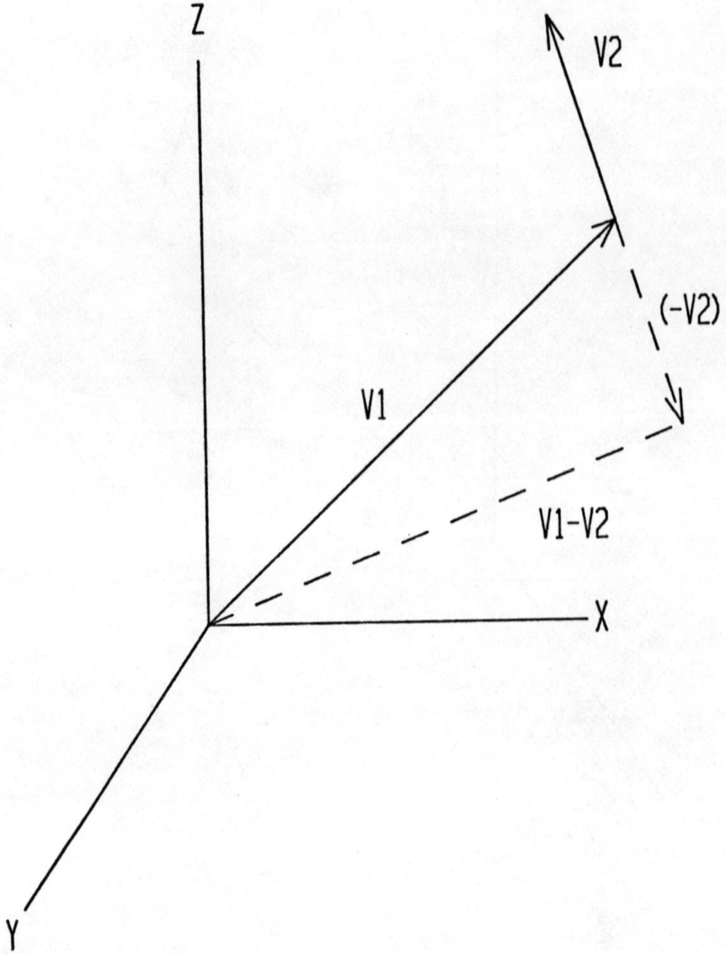

Fig. 47.

Vector Cross Product

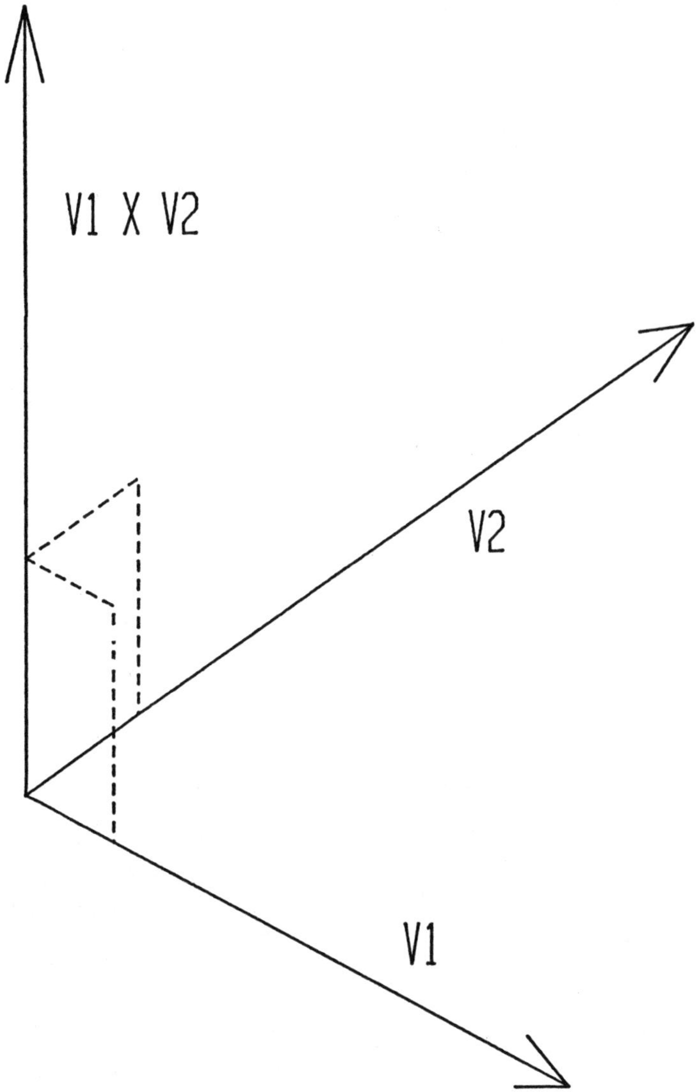

Fig. 48.

Dot Product

Dot product of two vectors is zero if they are orthogonal.

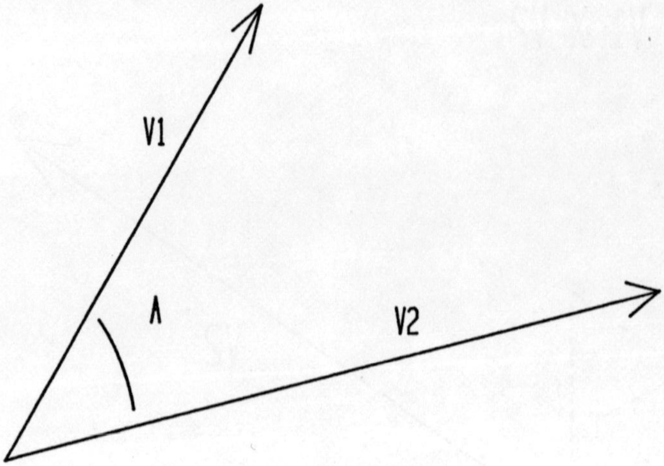

$A = 90^\circ$ if, and only if, $V1 \cdot V2 = 0$

Fig. 49.

Unit Vector

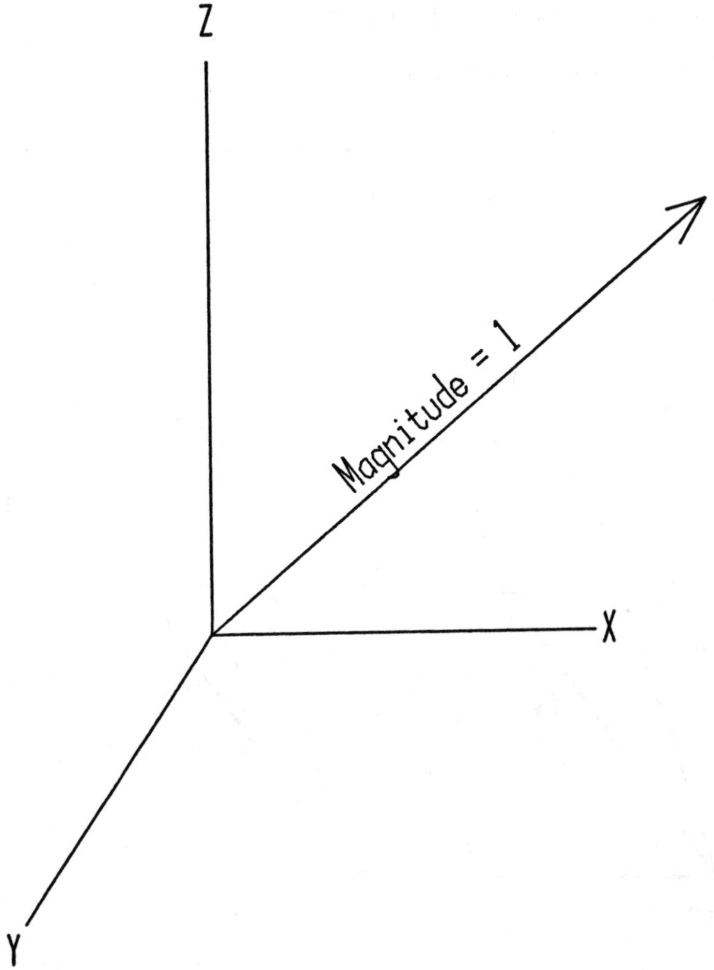

Fig. 50.

Scalar Triple Product

Interpreted as the volume of the parallelepiped with V1, V2, and V3 as adjacent edges ...

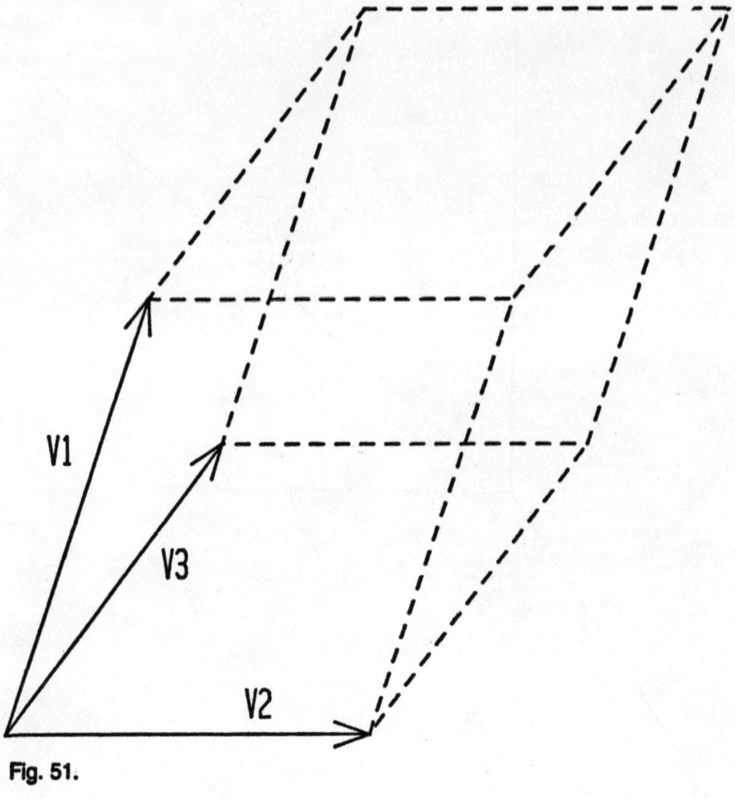

Fig. 51.

LISTING

```
10 "V+"GOSUB 200
    : A=A+D
    : B=B+E
    : C=C+F
    : GOTO 250
20 "V-"GOSUB 200
    : A=A-D
    : B=B-E
    : C=C-F
    : GOTO 250
30 "VC"GOSUB 200
    : Y=BF-CE
    : X=CD-AF
    : C=AE-BD
    : B=X
    : A=Y
    : GOTO 250
40 "VT"GOSUB 200
    : Y=ACS((AD+BE+CF) / √(AA+BB+CC) /
      √(DD+EE+FF))
    : Z$="THETA"
    : GOTO 260
50 "VD"GOSUB 200
    : Y=AD+BE+CF
    : Z$="DOT"
    : GOTO 260
60 "VM"GOSUB 230
    : Y= √(AA+BB+CC)
    : Z$="MAG"
    : GOTO 260
70 "VU"GOSUB 230
    : Y= √(AA+BB+CC)
    : A=A / Y
    : B=B / Y
    : C=C / Y
    : GOTO 250
80 "VK"GOSUB 230
    : INPUT"SCALAR K?",K
    : A=AK
    : B=BK
    : C=CK
```

```
: GOTO 250
 90 "STP"GOSUB 200
    : INPUT"I3?",G,"J3?",H,"K3?",I
100 Y=AEI+BFG+CDH-CEG-BDI-AFH
    : Z$="STP"
    : GOTO 260
200 INPUT"I1?",A,"J1?",B,"K1?",C
210 INPUT"I2?",D,"J2?",E,"K2?",F
220 RETURN
230 INPUT"I?",A,"J?",B,"K?",C
240 RETURN
250 PRINT"I= ";A
    : PRINT"J= ";B
    : PRINT"K= ";C
    : GOTO 1
260 PRINT Z$;"= ";Y
    : GOTO 1
```

Volume—Defined by Four Cartesian Space Points

This program computes the volume formed by connecting four points in space into a tetrahedron (Fig. 52) The four points must be expressed in rectangular notation (X,Y,Z). The volume is computed by the following formula.

$$\text{Volume} = \frac{1}{6}\begin{vmatrix} 1 & X1 & Y1 & Z1 \\ 1 & X2 & Y2 & Z2 \\ 1 & X3 & Y3 & Z3 \\ 1 & X4 & Y4 & Z4 \end{vmatrix}$$

Variables A through L are used for the values of the various X, Y, and Z coordinates. In line 10 these variables are addressed as array elements. In lines 20 and 30 these same variables are addressed by their letter names. As an example problem: What is the volume defined by the following four points in space?

(0,0,0) (1,0,0) (0,2,0) (0,0,3)

Display	You Enter
>>>	VS
X?	0
Y?	0
Z?	0
X?	1
Y?	0
Z?	0
X?	0
Y?	2
Z?	0
X?	0
Y?	0
Z?	3
VOL= 1.	ENTER
>>>	

Program length is 196 steps.

Volume ...

As defined by four cartesian space points.

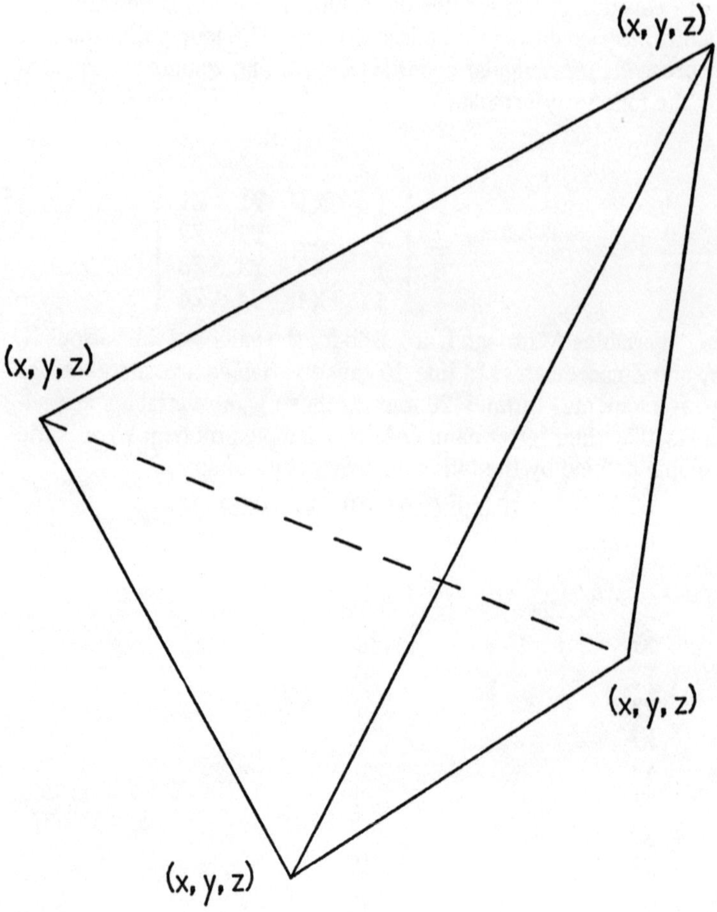

Fig. 52.

LISTING

```
10 "VS"FOR Z=1 TO 4
   : W=3Z-2
   : X=W+1
   : Y=3Z
   : INPUT"X?",A(W),"Y?",A(X),
   "Z?",A(Y)
   : NEXT Z
20 Q=AHL+BIJ+CGK-CHJ-BGL-AIK+
      AEI+BFG+CDH-CEG-BDI-AFH
30 R=DHL+EIJ+FGK-FHJ-EGL-DIK+
   AEL+BFJ+CDK-CEJ-BDL-AFK
40 V=ABS(Q-R) / 6
   : PRINT"VOL= ";V
   : GOTO 1
```

Wind Chill Index

This program computes the indicated wind chill index given the air temperature and the wind speed. For example: What is the wind chill index if the temperature is 32°F and the wind speed is 17 miles per hour?

Display	You Enter
> > >	WCI
TEMP? (F)	32
WIND? (MPH)	17
WIND CHILL = 9	ENTER
> > >	

If you prefer to work with Centigrade temperatures make the following changes to the program. First, change the value 91.4 to 33 in line 30 (two places). Then change the F to C in the input prompt of line 10.

Program length is 124 steps.

LISTING

```
10 "WCI"INPUT"TEMP? (F) ";T
20 INPUT"WIND? (MPH) ";W
30 X=91.4-(91.4-T)*(.474266+.303439* √W- .0202886W)
40 USING"# # # #"
   : PRINT"WIND CHILL = ";X
   : GOTO 1
```

Zero of a Function

This program finds a real root for any equation Y = f(X). The function should be programmed under label "FX" as in line 900 of the example. Successive values of X are input until the resulting Y value has a sign opposite that of the previous Y value. The program then automatically searches for the X value in the indicated interval where Y crosses zero, pausing temporarily with each iteration to display the narrowing interval. The two displayed numbers are values for X that approach each other.

The method used is bisection. The last two values for X define an interval that is cut in half with each iteration. This method guarantees a root in the interval and is fast enough for your pocket computer. For example: At what value of X is EXP(X) equal to 9? Write the equation so that solving for X at Y = 0 will yield our answer. Y = EXP(X) − 9 (Refer to Fig. 53). Program in this function under label "FX" and you're ready to go.

Display	You Enter
>>>	ZF
?	0
Y= −8.	
?	2
Y= −1.610943901	
?	3
Y= 11.08553692	
2. 3.	
2. 2.5	
2. 2.25	
2.125 2.25	
(after several iterations)	
2.197224577 2.197224578	ON
>>>	

Use the ON key to break the action. X will contain the most accurate solution so far. If your function has other roots, rerun the program using values for X near other suspected roots.
Program length is approximately 167 steps.

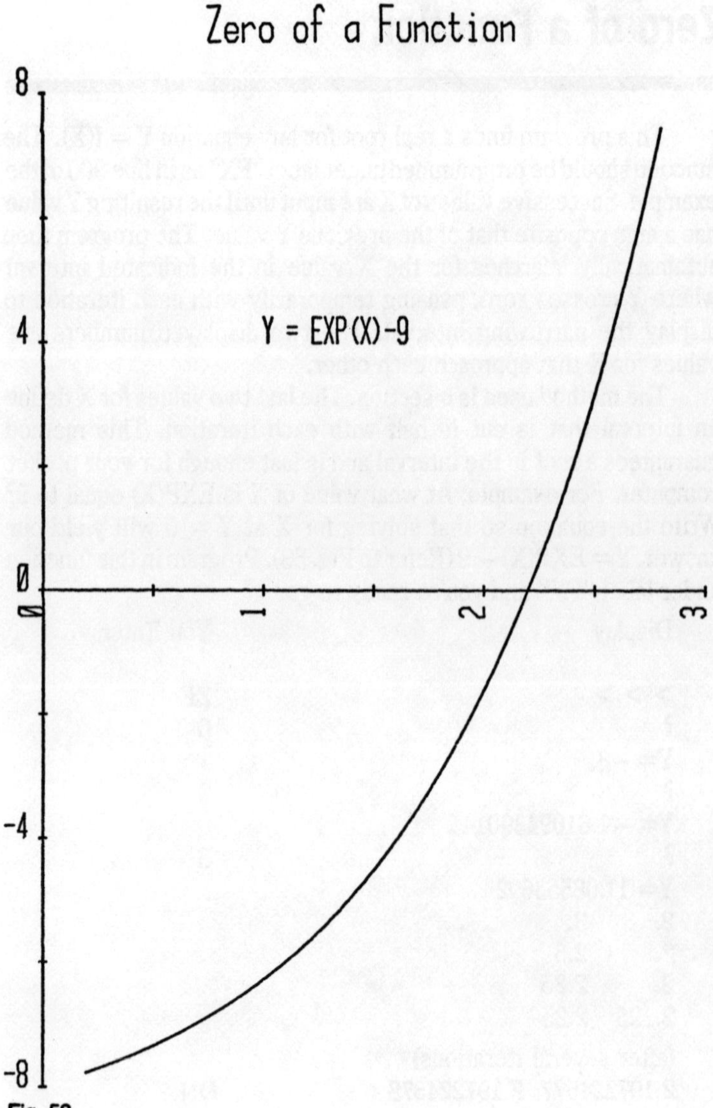

Fig. 53.

LISTING

```
 10 "ZF"X=0
    : Y=0
 20 A=X
    : B=Y
    : INPUT X
    : GOSUB"FX"
    : PAUSE"Y= ";Y
    : IF BY > = 0 THEN 20
 30 IF B < Y THEN 50
 40 D=B
    : C=A
    : B=Y
    : A=X
    : GOTO 60
 50 D=Y
    : C=X
 60 X=(A+C) / 2
    : PAUSE A,C
    : GOSUB"FX"
    : IF Y > 0 THEN 80
 70 B=Y
    : A=X
    : GOTO 60
 80 D=Y
    : C=X
    : GOTO 50
900 "FX"Y=EXP X-9
    : RETURN
```

Appendix A

TRS-80 Pocket Computer Reserved Words

Reserved Word	Shortest Abbreviation Allowed	
ABS	AB.	Absolute value
ACS	AC.	Inverse cosine
AREAD	A.	Data input
ASN	AS.	Inverse sine
ATN	AT.	Inverse tangent
BEEP	B.	Audible signal
CHAIN	CH.	Load and run from tape
CLEAR	CL.	Zero all variables
CLOAD	CLO.	Load program from tape
CLOAD?	CLO.?	Verify tape accuracy
CONT	C.	Continue program
COS	COS	Cosine
CSAVE	CS.	Store program on tape
DEBUG	D.	Program correction aid
DEG	DEG	Degrees (or hours) reformat
DEGREE	DEG.	Trigonometric mode
DMS	DM.	Degrees (or hours) reformat
END	E.	Terminate program
EXP	EX.	Exponential function
FOR	F.	Looping
GOSUB	GOS.	Subroutine call
GOTO	G.	Branching

Reserved Word	Shortest Abbreviation Allowed	
GRAD	GR.	Trigonometric mode
IF	IF	Decisional branching
INPUT	I.	Data input
INPUT#	I.#	Data load from tape
INT	INT	Integer function
LET	LE.	Assignment
LIST	L.	List program
LN	LN	Natural logarithm
LOG	LO.	Common logarithm
MEM	M.	Amount of unused memory
NEW	NEW	Erase program
NEXT	N.	Looping
PAUSE	PA.	Temporary data display
PRINT	P.	Display data
PRINT#	P.#	Store data to tape
RADIAN	RA.	Trigonometric mode
REM	REM	Comments
RETURN	RE.	Terminates subroutine
RUN	R.	Activate program
SGN	SG.	Sign function
SIN	SI.	Sine
STEP	STE.	Looping
STOP	S.	Halt program
TAN	TA.	Tangent
THEN	T.	Decisional branching
USING	U.	Data output formatting

THE KEYBOARD

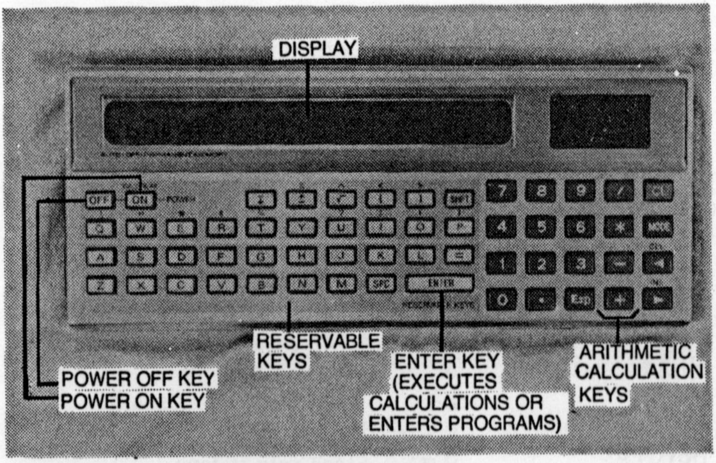

TRS-80 POCKET COMPUTER DISPLAYABLE SYMBOLS

A	/
B	*
C	-
D	+
E	(
F	)
G	√
H	π (SHFT up-arrow)
I	^ (SHFT √)
J	< (SHFT "(")
K	> (SHFT ")")
L	! (SHFT Q)
M	" (SHFT W)
N	# (SHFT E)
O	$ (SHFT R)
P	% (SHFT T)
Q	Y (SHFT Y, Yen sign)
R	? (SHFT U)
S	: (SHIFT I)
T	, (SHFT 0)
U	; (SHFT P)
V	=
W	
X	
Y	
Z	

Appendix B

Translating to Another BASIC

Here are a few quick checks to make as you translate programs from this book.

1. Use line numbers instead of labels.
2. Check for embedded logical tests. They are okay on some machines, but see Table B-1.
3. Renumber program lines as necessary.
4. Replace the square root and PI symbols if necessary.
5. Reformat the PRINT and PAUSE statements as appropriate for the target computer.
6. Put parenthesis around the arguments of built in functions. For example, rewrite SIN X as SIN (X).
7. Eliminate the implied multiplication of variables. For example, rewrite X=ABC as X=A*B*C.
8. Check the evaluation order of statements and insert parenthesis where necessary. For example, rewrite Y = √ AB*C as Y=SQR(A*B)*C.
9. Try several examples to verify the correct operation of your new program.

Let's take the program for finding prime numbers and rewrite it in a more standard BASIC format. Here's the Prime Numbers program as it appears in your TRS-80 Pocket Computer.

```
10: "PRI"INPUT "START N?",X:X=INT (X / 2)*2–1
20: X=X+2:Y=1
30: Y=Y+2: IF Y > √XPRINT X;" IS PRIME":GOTO 20
40: Z=X / Y:GOTO 30–10*(Z=INT Z)
```

ALTERNATE DEFINITIONS FOR A FEW TRS-80 POCKET COMPUTER FUNCTIONS

TRS-80	Function	Standard BASIC
Y=ABS X	Absolute value	10 LET Y=X 20 IF X < 0 LET Y=–X
Y=ACS X	Inverse cosine	10 Y=–ATN(X / SQR(1–X*X))+1.570796327
Y=ASN X	Inverse sine	10 Y=ATN(X / SQR(1–X*X))
Y=DEG X	Degrees (or hours), minutes, seconds format to decimal degrees (or hours)	10 H=INT(X) 20 M=100*(X–H) 30 S=100*(M–INT(M)) 40 Y=H+INT(M) / 60+S / 3600
DEGREE	Sets degree mode for all trigonometric functions	Most BASIC interpreters use radian mode exclusively. Convert angles as necessary. 10 R=D / 57.29577951 10 D=R*57.29577951
Y=DMS X	Decimal degrees (or hours) to degrees (or hours), minutes, seconds format	10 H=INT(X) 20 M=60*(X–H) 30 S=60*(M–INT(M)) 40 Y=H+INT(M) / 100+S / 100000
GRAD	Sets grad mode for all trigonometric functions	Most BASIC interpreters use radian mode exclusively. Convert angles as necessary. 10 R=G / 63.66197723 10 G=R*63.66197723
Y=LN X	Natural logarithm	10 Y=LOG(X)
Y=LOG X	Common logarithm	10 Y=LOG(X) / LOG(10)
PAUSE "HI"	Temporary halt of program to display data	10 PRINT "HI" 20 FOR I=1 TO 99 30 NEXT I (Adjust 99 for length of delay)
RADIAN	Sets radian mode for all trigonometric functions	Most BASIC interpreters use radian mode exclusively.
Y=SGN X	Sign of X	10 Y=0 20 IF X > 0 LET Y=1 30 IF X < 0 LET Y=–1 Usually, one of the following tricky statements will work correctly . . . 10 Y=(X > 0)–(X < 0) 10 Y=(X < 0)–(X > 0)
Y= $\sqrt{}$X	Square root	10 Y=SQR(X) (or . . .) 10 Y=X 20 Z=Y 30 Y=(Y+X / Y) / 2 40 IF Y< >Z THEN 20

Beginning with line 10, the first thing we must do is to drop the label "PRI". Then, for readability, the second statement of line 10 can be rewritten as line 12.

```
10 INPUT "START N?",X
12 X=INT(X / 2)*2–1
```

Line 20 is rewritten as two program lines.

```
20 X=X+2
22 Y=1
```

Line 30 needs a little more consideration if your version of BASIC won't handle multiple statements per line. Here's one approach . . .

```
30 Y=Y+2
32 IF Y > SQR(X) THEN 36
34 GOTO 40
36 PRINT X:" IS PRIME"
38 GOTO 20
```

Notice the square root function has been rewritten as a more conventional BASIC function.

Line 40 has two twists that need explaining. Inside the parenthesis is "Z=INT Z". Many versions of BASIC will allow you to make a logical test of this kind, although few programmers are aware of this fact. On your TRS-80 Pocket Computer a result of 1 is generated for true and 0 for false. So, if Z=INT Z is true, the computed value for everything inside the parenthesis of line 40 is a numerical 1. If Z=INT Z is false, the value is 0. As a result, if Z=INT Z then the program branches to line 20, otherwise the branch is to line 30.

```
40 Z=X / Y
42 IF X=INT(Z) THEN 20
44 GOTO 30
```

Now let's pull it all together, renumbering the program lines for neatness.

```
 10 INPUT "START N?",X
 20 X=INT(X / 2)*2–1
 30 X=X+2
 40 Y=1
 50 Y=Y+2
 60 IF Y > SQR (X) THEN 80
 70 GOTO 100
 80 PRINT X;" IS PRIME"
 90 GOTO 30
100 Z=X / Y
110 IF Z = INT(Z) THEN 30
120 GOTO 50
```

With a little practice, you'll find that most of the programs in this book are easy to translate.

Index

Edited by Dennis Thurlow

SAMOA	1.00
HONOLULU	2
S.FRANCISCO	5
ANCHORAGE	4
DENVER	6
CHICAGO	7
MANAGUA	6
MONTREAL	8
NEW YORK	8
BERMUDA	9
RIO JANEIRO	9
AZOREN	12
LONDON	13
LISSABON	13
DAKAR	12
STOCKHOLM	14
BERLIN	14
MADRID	14
HELSINKI	15
ATHEN	15
JOHANNESBURG	14
MOSKAU	16
NAIROBI	15
TEHERAN	15:30
BOMBAY	18:30
BANGKOK 21	19
PEKING HONKONG	21 — 20
TOKIO	21
SEOUL	21
SEDNEY	22
WELLINGTON	~~24~~ 00

W Szczebrzeszynie
Chrząszcz brzmi
w trzcinie.

In meinem
Hi-Ha-Haus
war eine Mi-
Ma-Maus.
Mi-Ma-Maus
raus aus meinem
Haus!

Der Mensch ist nur Mensch
durch die Sprache"
— W. Humboldt (1767-1835